MW01132746

...In Praise of 4FOUR BIG IDEAS

"4Four Big Ideas for the Future is a remarkable book written by an even more remarkable man. Jason's thoughtful, provocative, and compelling analysis of the effects of modern digital culture on the present and future of education brings entirely fresh perspectives to the field. His book is a thoroughly entertaining, even intoxicating read, **HIGHLY RECOMMENDED for anyone deeply concerned about the future of living and learning during digital times.**"

> — **Ian Jukes:** *CEO of Infosavvy21 and author of 17 books about educational innovation.*

"Dr. Jason Ohler once again informs, inspires, and entertains while connecting us with big ideas in accessible and practical ways. He generously shares wisdom gained across 35 years of engaging with students, teachers, musicians, artists, scientists – humans. This book is a pleasurable, inspiring journey **for EVERYONE living, learning and striving to accommodate myriad technological advancements and thrive as learner, parent, teacher and citizen.**"

> — **Karen Cator:** *CEO of Digital Promise, former Director of the Office of Education Technology for the US Department of Education.*

"Heartfelt, inspiring and beautifully written. The book blends the potential presented by emerging technologies with an unwavering long-term vision and commitment to student learning. Jason's clear insights and anecdotes provide readers with an engaging journey through the potential of modern education. I'd highly recommend you take the trip."

> — **Sam Gliksman:** *author of* The iPad in Education for Dummies, *and founder of the iPads in Education Ning community.*

"4Four Big Ideas for the Future is a thoroughly enjoyable read about the future of technology, learning, and living a digital lifestyle, that is packed with stories, insight and direction. **I highly recommend this book for anyone looking for practical and conceptual guidance for navigating the future.**"

> — **Shelly Palmer:** *Emmy-nominated Fox 5 New York's on-air tech expert, and a regular technology commentator for CNBC, MSNBC, CNN, and Fox Business News*

"Written in an engaging style, Ohler's work is replete with eye-opening insights into the new, blended lives we now live, straddling the boundary of the physical and online worlds. Filled with personal narratives about his relevant experiences in education, *4Four Big Ideas* **paints a fascinating portrait of modern culture that is relevant to us all.**"

> — **Alec Couros:** *Professor of educational technology and media at the Faculty of Education, University of Regina, Canada.*

"Jason has long spoken of real things…the power of digital story authoring, the complexities of digital citizenship, must-haves in reinvented education, art as the "fourth R," and other trends that we need to tune into. His insight inspires us to action. *4Four Big Ideas for the Future* **is the perfect piece at the perfect time."**

— **Kathleen Gradel:** *Professor in the College of Education, SUNY Fredonia, NY and is a recipient of the Chancellor's Award for Excellence in Teaching.*

"Dr. Ohler offers a thought-provoking roadmap for transforming the future of education, and convincingly argues this prospect is available now. **An inspiring and compelling call to action."**

— **Ed Madison:** *author of* Newsworthy, *a founding producer for CNN and a media producer for CBS, ABC, A&E, Paramount, Disney, and Discovery.*

"Jason Ohler excels at demystifying very complicated ideas in technology and education, and through his powerful and humorous way of telling stories, makes them very 'user-friendly', useful, and inspiring. **His actionable ideas will not only challenge your thinking, but will help you move forward in your own learning journey."**

— **George Couros:** *author of* The Innovator's Mindset: Empower Learning, Unleash Talent, *and* Lead a Culture of Creativity.

"Jason Ohler's *4Four Big Ideas for the Future* takes us on a lively, engaging and fascinating journey through a world that's part real, part digitally augmented reality and constantly changing. **This book is a blueprint for the kinds of deep and meaningful discussions needed to build the futures we want."**

— **Frank Gallagher:** *Vice President of the Education Cable Impacts Foundation*

"In *4Four Big Ideas for the Future* Jason Ohler escorts you, with great good humor, to the heart of every important question, from the future of text to digital citizenship to new technologies to the imperative of story, with no sign of triumphalist pretense or bombast, nor any hints of alarm. **Jason's straight-up wisdom and bullet-proof optimism makes you extremely glad that you've been along for the ride."**

— **Peter Gow:** *Executive Director of the Independent Curriculum Group.*

"Jason Ohler does a wonderful job breaking down the importance of educational technology in an accessible way for all educators. **This book is a must have for all teachers looking to dive deeper into the world of educational technology."**

— **Nicholas Provenzano:** *author of* Classroom in the Cloud.

"Jason Ohler's new book is **very engaging, full of stories based on decades of experience, and offers deep insight and practical advice for every educator. But the book isn't just for educators, it is for all of us."**

— **Becky Sipos:** *President & CEO of Character.org and CEO of the Character Education Partnership.*

"*4Four Big Ideas for the Future* extends Jason's perspective on a number of fronts, making clear the steps we need to take to make the most of the future. **This is a highly relevant, important, and very engaging read!**"

> — **Diana Graber:** *Co-Founder of Cyberwise.org and Founder of CyberCivics.com.*

"Thank God Jason received the medical miracle he needed to keep living. In turn he has provided **an excellent book that should be a must read for educators.** His experiences with technology are so real and full of insight, that everyone who finds technology challenging, particularly educators, will this find this book helpful. "

> — **Gary Bitter:** *Professor of Educational Technology in the Mary Lou Fulton Teachers College at Arizona State University, and Executive Director of Technology Based Learning & Research (TBLR).*

"Dr. Jason Ohler offers **a lifetime of wisdom** and again shows us his genius, as he explains our complex world in terms we can all understand, and that help us to become literate in today's 'now media' culture. Humorous, insightful, and riveting, Jason pinpoints for us what matters for students, and helps guide us to create a new learning ecology. **A must read for educational leaders everywhere.**"

> — **Mary Wegner:** *Superintendent, Sitka Alaska Schools, President Obama FutureReady Superintendents honoree, and member of the League of Innovative Schools.*

"Ohler has been a driving force of these changes for over 30 years. His new book, *4Four Big Ideas for the Future*, brings the breadth of his knowledge and insight to readers. **An inspiring must read for everyone.**"

> — **Mike Ribble:** *author of Digital Citizenship in Schools, 2nd Edition, and co-creator of the ISTE PLN on Digital Citizenship.*

"Jason Ohler is a scholar of transformation. He is a teacher of inspiration. He is a leader in learning. *4Four Big Ideas for the Future* helps us understand "digital age learning" via mobility, interconnection and a proliferation of information. However Ohler also shows us how to create digital citizenship with ethics, respect and integrity. **This is a remarkable book, written by a scholar whose stories and research transform our practice.**"

> — **Tara Brabazon:** *Professor of Education and Head of the School of Teacher Education at Charles Sturt University.*

"Dr. Ohler makes the complexities of our current educational and technological disruption both awe-inspiring and understandable, for educators and non-educators alike. *4Four Big Ideas for the Future* **offers excellent insights about where we are headed and still manages to bring it back to the basics. Most importantly, Dr. Ohler explains why humankind has a need for** creativity and storytelling - and always will - and how we can tell our own stories to shape the world the way we want."

> — **Marie Arturi:** *CEO/Founder eduBuncee*

Books by Dr. Jason Ohler...

Digital Storytelling in Education
New Media Pathways to Literacy, Learning and Creativity
A guide for blending the principles of effective storytelling and the tools of transmedia to tell engaging narrative for personal, educational and professional purposes.

Digital Community, Digital Citizen
An in-depth look at what it means to blend our real and virtual lives into one healthy, inspired approach to living.

Taming the Beast
Choice and Control in the Electronic Jungle
A guide for proactively assessing the impacts of technology on society, the environment and interpersonal relationships.

A Case Study of Online Community
The study that predicted Facebook and the world of online community.

Future Courses
A Compendium of Thought About Education, Technology and the Future
Kurzweil, Rheingold, Gates, Turkle and others weigh in on the future of learning and technology.

Then What?
Everyone's Guide to Living, Learning and Having Fun in the Digital Age
A roller coaster of a novel about how to survive a digitally overdone world in which schools must change if we are going to take back the future.

4Four BIG IDEAS

FOR THE FUTURE

understanding our innovative selves

by Jason Ohler

Brinton
·BOOKS·

4FOUR BIG IDEAS FOR THE FUTURE
Understanding Our Innovative Selves

© by Jason Ohler 2016

Published in the United States by Brinton Books

ISBN-13: 978-1522780335

ISBN-10: 1522780335

jasonOhlerIdeas.com

Cover and inside design by:
Larry Addington
2020 Design
Ashland, Oregon

For my wife, Saint Terri

· *In Grateful Acknowledgement* ·

of the anonymous organ donor whose foresight and
generosity saved my life

and of the medical staff at The Norton Thoracic Institute
and St. Joseph's Hospital in Phoenix, Arizona whose expertise
and care made it possible for me to breathe again.

CONTENTS

NEW TERMS FOR NOW MEDIA

· Glossary of Terms ·

ARt: Art created using Augmented Reality (AR).

Art the 4th R: Refers to the largely unrecognized fact that art has become a staple literacy for "reading and writing" across curricular areas, as well as for personal and professional pursuits. It highlights the fact that literacy involves more than just letters and numbers, and now embraces images, video, music, sound and emerging media forms, as well as the ability to combine a number of media forms in an articulate, aesthetic, professional manner.

Biposital: Synonymous with duotaneous. It refers to the blending of two things, activities or places at the same time. In this book it is used to describe blending the two worlds we simultaneously occupy, RL (real life) and IR (immersive reality), the world we access via our smart devices wherever we go.

Creatical thinking: Thinking that combines critical and creative thinking into one integrated problem identification and solving workflow process.

Detechtive: Someone committed to understanding the impacts of technology.

Duotaneous: Synonymous with biposital. It refers to the blending of two things, activities or places at the same time. In this book it is used to describe blending the two worlds we simultaneously occupy, RL (real life) and IR (immersive reality), the world we access via our smart devices wherever we go.

Edupreneur: An educator who innovates usually from within, and upon occasion from outside, the formal education system to create enterprising educational opportunities.

Hats vs. hat nots: Those who have "math hats," which neurologically augment our ability to do mathematics, vs. those who do not. This term is also used to distinguish those who possess any kind of neurologically enhancing wearable technology from those who do not. More broadly, it refers to the social and economic disparities that exist in such a situation. I first heard this term used by a high school student during a "You're In Charge" workshop.

Headware: Any neurological enhancement technology worn on the head.

iGlasses: A generic name for wearable, connected eyeglasses that typically have augmented reality capabilities.

IR: Immersive reality; the world on the other end of our smart devices that travels with us wherever we go.

iStuff: All of our "i" stuff, including hardware and apps.

Infopreneur: An entrepreneur who specializes in developing new enterprises in the world of data generation and analysis.

Infosphere: The secondary ecosystem in which we live, focused on information.

Mediascape: The secondary ecosystem in which we live, focused on multimedia and transmedia.

Mediasts: Those who make media.

Movicians: Movie artists.

Nowist: (Pronounced NOW-ist). One who is focused on what we could be doing right now, particularly in relation to social and educational change. A nowist stands in contrast to a futurist who speculates about what might be.

Now media: All the new media that seem to emerge unannounced. It is distinguished from new media, which has come to mean anything beyond print.

Online anthropology: The application of anthropological methodology to the study of virtual communities.

Ouriginal: A word used to describe work created using a mix of original, non-original and semi-original material. It describes the grey area of mashups and media collages.

Ouriginalize: To substantially adapt others' work to make it at least partly our own.

Partycipation: Pronounced just like "participation." It refers to attendance at the Internet party. It also refers more generally to the participatory nature of online social gatherings.

Screasel: A word combining screen and easel. This is where most of us draw and paint now.

Secording: Secretly recording people or events, usually with mobile personal devices.

Spinware, spinwear: Clothing or accessories specifically used to create an impression; often associated with pandering to the audience.

Subte(ch)**xt:** Pronounced just like "subtext." It refers to the often invisible backstory of technology, as well as its many unforeseen and unintended consequences.

Teachie: A teacher. The term is usually used to distinguish a teachie from a techie.

Te(ch)**xt:** Pronounced "text." Te(ch)xt is whatever form of communication output that is demanded by whatever medium we are using for expression.

tEcosystem: Our secondary ecosystem consisting of technology, data, the cloud and the communication they facilitate. Like our natural ecosystem, the tEcosystem consists of global, interdependent systems and subsystems. Unlike our primary ecosystem it can fail very quickly.

Transmersive: Combines transmedia and immersion. It's a term coined by media consultant Monica Helms.

U3W: The University of the World Wide Web, where we all go to school.

Wearware: Wearable technology, central to the BYOD (Bring Your Own Device) movement.

Webster: a retro term for one who does web work.

xTreme BYOD: BYOD stands for Bring Your Own Device; xTreme refers to the emerging edge of BYOD.

Why This Book?

This book is my attempt to capture the many inspirations that visited me during what I was sure was going to be my last year on the planet.

During that year I circled death's abyss, convinced by everything I read that the idiopathic pulmonary fibrosis (IPF) that had hijacked my lungs was going to kill me slowly and painfully.

As I sat plugged into oxygen 24/7, with my muscles atrophying and with many of the simple tasks of daily living beyond my grasp, I thought. A lot. I had been given a gift of inactivity that few ever receive, which had allowed me to see life, and particularly my thirty-five years as an educator, with great clarity. During that period of intense focus it became easy to separate noise from substance, and to see once again what drew me to a life of teaching and educational innovation. Simply put, there is no greater way that we, as a society and as individuals, can show our hope for the future than through how we educate our children and ourselves in the present. It is how our belief systems take shape, are tested and are made visible to the world. Being part of that effort for so many years had been an honor, and had allowed me to live a life that blended heart, soul and mind in purposeful activities that helped shape the present and touch the future in very real ways.

Above all, my life as an educator had allowed me to help thousands of people become heroes of their learning stories, and craft lives that looked beyond their devices and toward community enrichment and personal fulfillment. The time I spent huddled around my oxygen concentrator was a time of many epiphanies, and while I didn't expect to be able to do anything with them, I was grateful simply for having had the opportunity to have them visit me in the privacy of my own thoughts.

Then came the double lung transplant that literally breathed new life into my nearly expired body, just in the nick of time. I was given another gift of time, but in this case it was in the form of longevity that I hadn't expected and which had allowed me to write this book. I hope my insights are helpful to readers in real ways that allow them to reshape their attitudes toward learning, community and living a technological lifestyle. And I hope it helps them place their digitally deluged lives into some kind of perspective. At the end of the day, we all want a more humane world that honors human potential. We want a world that channels our innately innovative selves into creating the futures we want and which can sustain us spiritually, intellectually, emotionally and physically. I hope that in some small way, this book can help others have big ideas so they can build those futures. And I hope the futures they build are creative, reflective and worthy of their imaginations.

Who Is This Book For?

Everyone.

It is for everyone who wants to understand our media-saturated age, and how to blend the two realities we all call home: real life and immersive reality, that second environment on the other end of our smart devices that travels with us wherever we go.

It is for everyone who wants to understand that we are living in a new literacy and communication landscape that goes far beyond facility with letters and numbers, and embraces the media collage and all the emerging "now" media coming our way. This new landscape is not just for students; it is for everyone. Or, it is for students and we are all students. Take your pick.

It is for everyone who wants to understand what it means to be truly educated, and why that means we must not only follow our passions but also be reflective about our passions, and cultivate a big-picture perspective as digital citizens.

It is for everyone who wants to understand where major technology trends are headed, and how we might steer the direction of what has become an out-of-control roller coaster with no braking system, so that we can create the learning environments, communities and lives we truly want.

And it is for everyone who wants to know how to cut through all the noise that swirls around us so that we can own our own stories, and tell them clearly, with humanity and authenticity. I know only one thing for certain about the technologies that await us in the future: we will find ways to tell stories with them. Let's make sure they are the stories we want the world to hear.

This book is for everyone.

What Is This Book?

The material in this book is based on four of Dr. Ohler's most highly regarded presentations. It consists of syntheses or mashups, if you will, of these presentations and his many experiences as an educational technologist during his lifetime as a learning innovator. Every attempt has been made to maintain the conversational nature of his presentations, while adapting them to the written medium. The 4Four big ideas presented in this book are massaged by reflection, artistic license and the sense of fun he developed over the years as an antidote to the possible despair and anxiety one can develop while trying to commandeer the technology juggernaut, which seems exciting and terrifying at the same.

Even though he approaches this book primarily as an educator, his work with business, research, mental health and a number of other areas deeply informs his message. Besides, as he will note throughout the book, the lines between school, home, learning, life, work and play are so blurred at this point that to discuss one of them is to discuss all of them. The digital, ubiquitous, mobile domain is the umbrella under which everything happens. The distinctions we make among the many activities in our lives are largely a matter of conversational convenience, not reality.

Regardless of what you do for a living, or how you pursue your personal passions, this book will help you understand the age you are living in as one that is roiling with change, opportunity and caution. It will also help you understand that being innovative is our natural state, a fact that emerging forms of technological and media expression simply amplifies.

About the Author

Jason Ohler is a professor emeritus and President's Distinguished Professor of educational technology and virtual learning. Jason has been telling stories about the future that are rooted in the realities of the past during the entire thirty five years he has been involved in the world of innovative education. He is also a lifelong digital humanist who is well known for the passion, insight and humor that he brings to his presentations, projects and publications.

He has worked both online and in classrooms, at home and internationally, for over three decades helping students develop the new literacies they need to be successful in the digital age. He is a passionate promoter of "Art the 4th R" and of creatical thinking, combining critical and creative thinking into one integrated workflow.

He is also an enthusiastic champion of the need for everyone to learn how to use technology wisely and safely, with awareness and compassion, so they can become informed and productive citizens in a global, connected society. Above all, he has spent his many years in education combining innovation, creatical thinking and digital know-how to help renew and reinvent teaching and learning.

He has won numerous awards for his work and is author of many books, articles and online resources.

Many call him a futurist, he calls himself a nowist, believing we already have what we need to create the kinds of communities we need in order to meet the challenges of the digital age with creativity and humanity. His last book, *Digital Community, Digital Citizen,* explores the issues of helping our students blend their digital and non-digital lives into one, healthy, integrated approach to living. His book, *Digital Storytelling in the Classroom,* helps students become heroes of their own life stories, and speak the language of new media with clarity and humanity.

"The goal is the effective, creative and wise use of technology . . . to bring together technology, community and learning in ways that meet our needs as human beings. And while we are at it, to have fun."

FOREWORD

Yong Zhao

University of Oregon

This book is a gift from heaven, a miracle performed by the technology god.

The chance for me to write the foreword for this book was non-existent when I last saw the author merely a few months ago. Jason Ohler and I presented together to a group of educators and community members in beautiful Sitka, Alaska. I was there in person and Jason came in via Skype from Arizona. I was told that Jason was very ill, in fact, terminally ill. Jason was in a chair, visibly weak, but delivered a stunning presentation. It could have been one of his last great presentations because his lungs were losing capacity due to a disease called idiopathic pulmonary fibrosis.

That was February 2015. Then in November, I received an email from Jason asking if I would write the foreword for his new book. I was beyond surprised: How is it possible for someone who was facing death to have written a book?

Jason had a double lung transplant, as I later learned. Thanks to a generous donor and modern medical technology, Jason has a pair of new lungs. And he is back, with a powerful book.

I have been a fan of Jason's work for a long time, ever since I read his book *Taming the Beast: Choice and Control in the Electronic Jungle* in 1999. Jason lives with technology, uses technology, champions for technology, and seems to love technology, but he is not a technocrat. He is a humanist, someone who values the agency and interest of human beings. He wants technology to serve the human interest, not to control human beings. Jason is a philosopher, who appreciates the power and potential of technology in creating changes, changes that force human beings to adapt. At the same time, he also understands that humans have the capacity to change, to take control, to decide when, why, where, and how to use technology appropriately and wisely. Moreover, Jason is an educator, a reflective one who has taught at different levels. As a result, his writings are always insightful and inspiring, deeply grounded in educational practices.

More importantly, Jason has the amazing ability to see the big picture, the forest, so to speak. In the technology jungle are many entangling trees that are constantly growing and dying. Technological inventions come and go. Brilliant (and not so brilliant) ideas become popular and then vanish quickly. Contradictory and conflicting suggestions are offered constantly to teachers, parents, students, and policy makers. But Jason has always been able to figure out what's important and present his observations and insights succinctly.

Jason is about big ideas. In this new book, Jason brings his life's work together and offers four big ideas for the future. While no one can predict what the future will be, it seems reasonable to believe that we will live in a world drastically different from the past. One aspect of that world is the multiple realities created by technology. There is little doubt that our life will increasingly be mediated by technological devices that are extremely powerful in connecting with fellow human beings, distorting or enhancing our senses, and providing or overwhelming us with information. This new world is also constantly changing in unexpected ways.

What is required of us to live in this future world will naturally be different from what we knew in the past. To thrive in, or even to cope with our new world we will need to develop new literacies, reconsider citizenship and ethics, understand how things may change, and grow our ability to tell stories with new media. But most important, Jason suggests, we need to be creative, inventive, and entrepreneurial. We must reinvent ourselves. Luckily, the humanist Jason Ohler believes that as human beings, we can do all of that if and when we understand and accept the imperative to change.

This book continues the Jason Ohler tradition of writing—insightful, inspiring, humorous, practical, and straightforward. But it is even more candid, passionate, and almost impatient because his experience with the life-threatening disease has taught him the real meaning of the saying: life is brief and fragile.

4our BIG IDEAS FOR THE FUTURE

Once I was attending a conference when I heard a keynote speaker declare that lecture was dead. He was so convincing that I got up and left.

I know only one thing for certain about the technologies that await us in the future: We will find ways to tell stories with them. Let's tell stories that are inspiring, thoughtful and worthy of our imaginations.

Because the future is just getting started.

IDEA 1

WRITING TECHXT

Now Media, New Literacies

I once heard a keynote speaker declare that lecture was dead and never sense the irony in his statement. He was so convincing that I got up and left. On my way towards the exit I heard him declare his love for TED talks. Again, no sense of irony. I also heard him implore the audience to buy his book about the death of books, and to travel half way around the world to attend his conference about the effectiveness of online conferences. And as I pushed through the double doors in the back of the auditorium, I heard him say, "And the wonderful thing about individualized learning is that it is so collaborative in nature."

We are walking, talking contradictions, so awash in competing pedagogies, technologies and philosophies that we are bound to bump into ourselves sooner or later. When we do, we are left to wonder what we're really doing and why we are doing it. Right up front, let me offer an important piece of advice, which was passed on to me long ago by educator Don Shalvey: Beware the paradigm du jour. You can have the most pedagogically flipped, globally flat, intrinsically motivating, expertly scaffolded, STEM-based, data-driven, over-tested, peer-assessed, technology-infused, engaging, participatory, authentic, blended, differentiated program in the world. However, at the end of the day the focus has to be on student learning in the deepest and broadest sense, regardless of our latest educational enamorment. Continually, we need to ask the same question that a recent U.S. president asked: Is our children learning? Good question. Is they? More importantly, what are they learning? That is, how have we defined being an educated person at this point in history?

If you want to test your commitment to student learning, then try challenging yourself at your next meeting to begin your comments with, "In order to better serve students" and see what happens. Then try challenging others at the table to do the same–but I'd wait until you have tenure. You're bound to ruffle some feathers. Focusing on student learning is your captain's wheel and rudder as you navigate social and technological seas that are roiling with change. Using student learning as a focal point might seem too obvious to point out, but I assure you that in our high-stakes testing culture it is often overlooked.

The reality is that the innovation instinct that is so natural to us has become a roller coaster without brakes. It is up to each of us, but particularly those of us in education, to steer it in the direction toward helping students develop the skills and perspectives they need to create solutions to the challenges that face their local, global and digital communities. Bottom line: We need to continually ask ourselves what it means to be an educated person. And we need to understand that the answer to that question changes as technology changes.

And now, if I might, I would like to get serious for a moment. And get very personal. Then on with the show.

I am 63, but my lungs are less than half that age. In the spring of 2014 I was diagnosed with idiopathic pulmonary fibrosis–IPF for short. Idiopathic simply means that we have no idea what causes something. So, you can have an idiopathic toothache or leg cramp that defies diagnosis. You can also have an idiopathic career or marriage. I'd watch out for that.

Pulmonary fibrosis is a progressive disease that scars over the lungs, choking off the mechanisms the lungs use to absorb and distribute oxygen and exchange it for carbon dioxide. Slowly, those with IPF suffocate from oxygen deprivation and are poisoned by their inability to expel CO_2. By the summer of 2014 I had become a balloon with a slow leak. I was plugged into oxygen 24-7. Simple movements, like taking a shower, or retrieving a pen I dropped on the floor, required help.

IPF kills most who get it, slowly and painfully. But at the eleventh hour I received the only reprieve available to me: a double lung transplant. Due to the foresight and generosity of a stranger, as well as groundbreaking technology and a medical

4

team with uncanny expertise, I am able to be here with you today. Like all miracles, the entire experience was humbling, recalibrating and ultimately inspiring.

However, for nearly a year I circled the abyss, pretty much convinced from everything I read that I too was going to die a slow and painful death. I was saying my good-byes to friends, making peace with old girlfriends, making sure I told those close to me that I loved them, and apologizing for not having told them often and clearly enough in the past. I settled in for the downward slide, to be taken care of by my wife, whose kindness and patience transcended friendship and entered the realm of saintliness. If you would like to read about my inspirations and revelations on the journey from IPF to transplant, go to *realbeing.me*.

During that year, it became increasingly difficult for me to manage simple movement, so I sat, as my muscles atrophied, and I reflected. A lot. I will spare you the more ethereal reflections, except to say that prior to my illness I, like all of you, understood that life was fragile and brief. However, that year I felt it on a cellular level and with a sense of depth and connectedness that extended far beyond my normal reality. Much to my amazement, I decided that I liked the fact that life was so fragile and brief. That's what made it so special.

Yet, what's truly important here are my reflections on my life as an educator. Or perhaps a better place to start is to tell you what I didn't think about. I didn't think to myself, "Gosh, I wish I had given students more tests," or gone to more meetings, or followed the educational standards more closely. Those kinds of considerations receded into the background as unnecessary noise. Instead, I found myself hoping I had been as good an educator as Miss Phelps, my 1st and 2nd grade teacher.

The year of this photo of Miss Phelps and myself, as best as I can determine, is 1958. During the 1950s all second grade teachers looked perpetually sixty-five years old. As you can see,

Miss Phelps did not disappoint in this regard. Notice the white shirt buttoned all the way up the chest. She put so much commercial grade starch in her shirts that when she hugged me it sounded like cellophane crinkling. During the sweltering heat of a Western New York summer day, she would still wear wool skirts half way down her calves. It was the proper thing to do.

But don't let her austere countenance mislead you. She was a ninja teacher with a glint in her eye, a heart of gold and tremendous teaching talent. She had everyone fooled. She looked conservative, but when the door closed, she went about the business of student learning with a passion that belied her appearance. She had infiltrated the system. I adored her. All her students adored her. I couldn't wait to get to school.

She was also a great educational technologist. She leveraged students' interests by using all of the technology at her disposal: finger paints, books, 45 RPM records, building blocks, toys, those big fat crayons that came eight in a box, you name it. She used the technology of the day to help students learn as much as they could, as enjoyably as they could.

Most importantly, she was a door opener. Rather than insist that every student pass through a standardized learning door, she looked for a special learning door for each student. Then she delighted in opening it and in helping each student embark on a personalized learning journey.

Above all, she used her special talents like an expert. I will never forget something that happened during a unit she was teaching on dinosaurs. I was having a hard time memorizing dinosaur names, and was becoming frustrated, when she said,

"Jason, you like to tell stories. Why don't you name them and tell stories about them?" So, that's exactly what I did. Ever since then, two in particular have been with me throughout my life: Stegosaurus Stan and Tyrannosaurus Tom.

There are two take-aways here. First, notice how skillfully Miss Phelps adapted my interests and skills to the lesson of the day. She was a great door opener and a true teacher in this regard. And second, notice how successfully storytelling works in education. Fifty years later, I remember these dinosaurs well. But beyond her skills as an educator, I remember Miss Phelps most for the soulful gleam in her eye she had every day that said, "Come on in, let's do an end run around the system, open some doors, have some fun and learn everything we can." God bless Miss Phelps. Thanks to her and two wonderful parents, I had a Disney childhood.

That year, as I sat huddled around my oxygen machine, I also found myself hoping that I had been as good a teacher as Mr. Hasselback. He's in the picture on the left, and that's me playing bass  guitar on the right. I was in 10th grade when Mr. Hasselback opened a very important door for me: the music door.

This was the 1960s. The counter culture was exploding. Music was in a state of revolution, from Joni Mitchell to Jimi Hendrix to Blood Sweat and Tears. It was the time in global history known as Beatlemania. For Gen Xers and beyond, you will have to talk to an old person or consult the oracle YouTube to find out more about Beatlemania. It was absolutely amazing.

For me, it was one of the first international, blockbuster media campaigns that brought together celebrity, big guitar amplifiers, huge rock 'n' roll stadiums, TV, radio, fan mags and the whole nine yards. All the attention was focused on four guys from Liverpool who made our parents apoplectic because they had "long hair," which meant that their bangs swooped down and brushed the tops of their eyebrows. Keep in mind that they didn't have sideburns of any magnitude and their ears were clearly visible. But the bangs alone were a radical shift from the standard-issue crew cut of the day. Predictably, every guy who wanted any kind of social life wanted to look like a Beatle. Exasperated parents and their defiant kids spent hours locked in heated battle about hairstyle, particularly about who could dictate hairstyle: Youth? Parents? Schools? The arguments that raged were symbolic of a widely felt angst about the extreme changes brought on by the counter culture revolution, during which youth directly challenged authority about everything from politics to personal hygiene. Needless to say, colored hair, nose piercings, tattoos, even girls dressed in anything but dresses and skirts, were many years off. It was a different time.

The newsreels about Beatlemania were riveting. My buddies and I watched in awe as women at Beatle concerts listened to a minute of music, and then screamed and passed out. The spectacle set our adolescent minds ablaze. We raced off to the local musical instrument store in my parents' Rambler station wagon, bound and determined not to let our lack of talent stop us in our quest to become rock stars. That was back in the day when you didn't need to be good, you just needed to be loud. There was a lot of bad, loud music back then. I'm afraid I contributed to it.

However, I actually had talent. I still have it, although I don't have it as much in my fingers as I do in my ears. Beginning at a young age, I have had the ability to listen to most popular songs and figure them out by plunking around on the piano. I had developed my own system for understanding music which came quite naturally to me. I think Howard Gardner might call my abilities musical intelligence.

So, it's 1968. I'm in 10th grade. I was in a rock 'n' roll band, as I had been for a number of years, mostly to get girls to like me. But by 10th grade I had really fallen in love with music. I had transformed into a real musician. I didn't really care that much about what being in a band did for my social life anymore. I wanted to play music for a living.

Enter Mr. Hasselback. He was offering a music theory course that I knew, in my bones, would take me to the next step in my musical development. I remember reading the course description and feeling my heart light up. His course was exactly what I needed. However, there was a hitch. A prerequisite for the course stipulated that students had to be able to read music. I couldn't. I understood the musical notation system, probably the way most of you do. I could use that old mnemonic "Every Good Boy Deserves Fudge" to figure out what notes to play. But by the time I had, the song was over. I simply had not done the hard work of developing the automaticity needed to actually read and play music in real time. My heart sank.

But I didn't give up. I went to Mr. Hasselback and I said, "Here's the thing. I can't read music but I think I can hear music." He said, "Okay, what does that mean?" I explained to him about being able to sit at a piano and figure out songs, and I showed him the system I had developed based on popular music. He looked at me quizzically and then finally said, "Okay, it's a bit unorthodox, but I will give you a listening test to evaluate your understanding of note relationships. If you can pass the listening test, I will let you into my class." I passed the listening test, enrolled in the class and I got one of the best grades that semester. I did better than Marcia, the piccolo player, who really didn't want me in the class because I wasn't in the "reading music club." I know I should forgive and forget, but if I were to see Marcia today I think I would still tell her, "neener, neener."

Thanks to Mr. Hasselback opening that music door for me, I have written symphonic music, string quartets, edgy electronic music, jazz... you name it. Most of the music that's heard playing in the background before my public presentations is original. I have also played in my share of bands, which have been some of my favorite adventures. I still sit at the piano and play for hours, figuring out music and writing my own. Above all, music is very therapeutic. And much cheaper than seeing a therapist. You can go to jasonohler.com/music, and listen to my music. You can even download original ringtones I've created. They're free.

The point is that when the system said that I had to be able to read music, Mr. Hasselback said, "I don't care what the system says. I'm going to let this student learn." He used an alternative approach to assessing my abilities that opened a door for me that he didn't have to open. Any administrator in any school district would have supported his right to demand that reading music be required of all students who wanted to take his music theory course. But he didn't demand this of me. As a result of his open-mindedness and commitment to student learning, I have had a life of music. God bless you, Mr. Hasselback, for being a door opener.

Bottom line? There are two. First, don't wait to get a life threatening illness to think about what is truly important to you, as a parent, an educator, a professional, a human being. Think about it now. Let those reflections guide you now. Live each day as though it were your first, and your last. Act now, in the moment, but with a long view, with the understanding that every action echoes for an eternity.

Second, be a door opener. Remember that you are always a teacher, no matter what you do for a living or wherever you find yourself, whether in a classroom, a boardroom, a dining room, an office environment or an online community. You teach others directly through your counsel and example, as well as indirectly by how you behave towards them. Teach mindfully. If you are a professional educator, then be an activist educator. Find out your students', employees' or colleagues' passions, and then open doors for them. They will be happier. And so will you. Teachers occupy that sacred interface between students, their imaginations and the world, and we either listen to our students and open doors for them, or we don't. When we don't, everybody loses, including us.

Most importantly, if you spend your life opening doors then you will enter retirement without misgivings. My father was a teacher for his entire working career, from the day he left the army after World War II until cancer claimed his life in 1972. On his deathbed he told me that other than not getting to spend more time with his family, he had no regrets. He loved opening doors for students every day of his life. And he told me something I will never forget: Get a job you love and never go to work again. That's what he did. I have lived by that advice and it has served me well. I recommend it to you.

He also told me, "When confronted by jerks, just remember, it could be worse: You could be one of them." Also wise words, but that's another story.

Here's the point. For us, opening doors has never been as important as it is now. Our students are banging on the schoolhouse door these days saying, "If you will just let us in with our mashups, digital stories, games, animations and all those things we know how to do, then we will show you what we know. We will show you how we learn. We will show you things you might like to learn." Unfortunately, that door is often closed to them, because high-stakes testing discourages it, incentives don't exist to encourage it or some are just too complacent, stubborn or honestly happy with the status quo to consider it. Nobody wins in this situation. Our students need our wisdom and experience, and we need their understanding of digital lifestyles and the new media landscape. We have a wonderful opportunity to collaborate. But we, the adults, need to let it happen. We control the door. Open the door and see what happens. It will change your life.

Thanks for allowing me a philosophical moment. Now, on with the show.

Eight Building Blocks of Modern Education

The title of this talk is *Writing Te(ch)xt- Now Media, New Literacies.* I will explain those terms a little later. But first, let me paint a big picture background that will be helpful.

In this presentation I am going to explore the issue of learning and literacy in a rapidly evolving educational media culture by addressing some of the building blocks of modern education. There are many building blocks, and which I emphasize depends on whom I am addressing. For you, I have selected the following eight: 1) being mobile, 2) being massively and richly interconnected, 3) shifting from text to media collage–that is, *writing techxt (pronounced "text")*, 4) adopting Art as the 4th R, 5) valuing writing, 6) seeing the world through the lens of digital citizenship and 7) harnessing stories not only to increase effective leadership, learning and communication, but also to visualize the futures we want for ourselves and our communities. Building block eight is a surprise.

In the spirit of full disclosure, I need to warn you not to let my structured approach fool you. It is just a smokescreen that allows me to jam everything I have learned about digital age learning during the last thirty-five years into the space of an hour. I will admit right up front that I am going to break the cardinal rule of speaking: I am going to make far too many points. After all, if you go to a keynote speaking school, and surely such a school must exist, you will learn that you should only make three main points. That is all the audience can absorb. I take a slightly different approach. I am going to make three thousand points and let you choose the three you like. I think it's more democratic.

On to building block number one.

Building Block 1: Being Mobile

It sounds almost cliché to point out the fact that we are mobile, but don't lose your historical perspective here. The idea that we would always carry our phones with us, and that they would seamlessly connect us to each other and the World Wide Web wherever we went, was science fiction not long ago. We are just at the very beginning of figuring out how to use the power of mobility in education, and the future is just getting started.

Building Block 2: Being Massively and Richly Interconnected

We are massively and richly interconnected to each other and to quality resources in ways that we couldn't imagine ten years ago. This has opened up access to an extraordinary world of learning opportunities, many of which are free or inexpensive, and easy to use. These learning opportunities will only increase in the years to come.

Let's consider the combined effect of being mobile and interconnected. Their confluence creates an alternative existence that travels with us wherever we go. We now all live in two places at once, at every moment. First, we live in real life, or RL, as we now refer to it. Once simply referred to as "life," we have had to rename it in order to distinguish it from the second place we now live, IR, or immersive reality. I am using the term "immersive reality" differently than it is typically used within the commercial world, which has branded it largely for entertainment purposes. Instead, I use the term more generally to refer to the ubiquitous, continuous, parallel universe on the other end of our smart devices that provides integrated functionality for every aspect of our lives. Our devices are, to quote MIT's Sherry Turkle, "always on and always on us," immersing us in a secondary source of information and a secondary sense of place, wherever we are. Burn this into your psyche: Living in two places at once is our new home.

What do we call this truly new existence? If we were academics, we might create a new word with a Latin root, and call it something like bipostal or duotaneous. Yet, the reality is that living in two places at once is simply the new normal. We don't even think about it.

All of this might bother some of you. You might think, "I don't have to live in two places. I can just turn my device off." But here's the reality: *you aren't going to.*

None of us are going to turn off our smart device for any length of time, unless maybe we're camping, or having family downtime, or making good on a bet. Think about it. How much would someone have to bet you to turn off your cell phone for a day? We expect each other to keep our phones on. We consider each other socially irresponsible if our phones are not turned on. Suppose one of your kids calls, needs help and you are having a philosophical moment about being off the grid. How guilty would you feel? Living in real life and immersive reality–duotaneously, if you will–is now the new normal.

Let's consider some of the implications of living in two places at once. In another presentation, *Five Trends that Bend,* I look at these effects very broadly. Here I just want to focus on what they mean for education.

One implication comes in the form of a question: Do we want our students to live two lives or one? Our immersive realities bridge our worlds of school, work and life. Yet many students live two lives–a non-digital life at school and a digital life outside of school. They go to school, turn off their devices and then turn them on again after school, or during study hall, or when we're not looking. We can either help our students integrate their two lives, or leave them to do it without our guidance. Our goal should be to help them blend both lives into one integrated, inspired, responsible approach to life. History will judge us based on how well we helped them achieve this goal. To make this happen, we have to open the door.

Another implication of being mobile and massively interconnected is that our new, immersive environment provides a broad continuum of educational experience for all learners wherever they are, wherever they go, whatever their needs. On one end of this continuum is mass personalization. The materials on the Web are so good that affordable, quality, personalized learning has finally arrived. Each student can have a very individualized approach to learning that's tailored to her specific needs and strengths. On the other end of the spectrum is selective participation. Students can join learning teams from all over the world and work as collaboratively as they want. We can connect students from Iceland, Alaska and Louisiana to study global warming, or to compare and contrast the differences in local cultures and customs. Along the continuum are options that combine the best of both worlds, allowing students to mix personal pursuits with participatory pedagogy. They can maintain these connections wherever they are. The possibilities are rich, varied and continually evolving.

This leads us to another implication that comes in the form of a question: Where is school? It's a variation of a question I heard Marshall McLuhan ask when I was a student in his classroom at the University of Toronto: When the information outside school exceeds the information within school, doesn't school interfere with our education? In 1977, he coauthored a book with his son, Eric, and Kathryn Hutchon titled, *City as Classroom,* in which he encouraged educators to expand the information sources they used with students to include modern media, as well as their immediate communities. Note that he was not referring just to media, but also to the physical world outside of school: IR and RL. Both offered the possibilities of extending traditional school. It was a radical notion at the time and prescient for us given our current immersive environment. Today, we are living this possibility. Wherever we go we live in two immediate environments, both of which provide rich learning opportunities. Combining them is becoming an art form, as well as a way of life.

City as Classroom reminds us that our mobility makes real life a valuable learning resource. We can treat whatever students do, wherever students are, as extensions of school if we ask them to mine their activities, combine them with research, and create reflective, well documented narratives about their experiences. Visiting a museum, exploring a local ecosystem, attending a political rally, shadowing someone at a business, or even just watching a movie or observing people at the mall, all qualify as extensions of the classroom. Supplementing RL activities with the resources of IR provides a powerful approach to learning. Of course, in order for these activities to qualify as school we would need to open a door.

One of the most valuable skills we should be teaching students is how to use their local communities and the World Wide Web as a school *while they are still at school.* Remember this: The attitude is the aptitude. Our intelligence is determined, at least in part, by our curiosity and the degree to which we enjoy learning. This has always been true to some extent. Now it is crucial. We should be helping students develop their own narratives, projects, reports and documentaries focused on their interests and passions. They will be teaching themselves and going to the University of the World Wide Web, or U3W, for the rest of their lives. We should help them do it well. We want them to be able to mine and synthesize data intelligently. We want them to be able to prepare their own learning processes and materials that are articulate, research based, professional and sharable. Understanding the nature of information and being able to teach themselves effectively are the skills they will need above all others.

Another implication of being mobile and immersed is that education is now largely a buyer's market, especially in higher education. This is a relatively new development. In more traditional models, colleges and universities were gatekeepers, allowing access to learning resources to only a select few. Everyone else was left to forage whatever education they could from the limited options available to them. Not anymore. There are many online universities, as well as bricks-and-clicks blended institutions that require limited residencies. Those who think the whole "degree thing" is silly can simply attend U3W, as they need to, as their learning goals evolve. Immersion has created an intense competition for our learning attention.

I'm often asked what I think about the fate of the university degree. Having spent 35 years in higher education, I have a few ideas about this topic.

I think that having a university degree will be seen as valuable for many years to come. However, the value of a degree will depend on how universities recognize their basic currency, the course credit. The current movement known as Competency Based Education, or CBE, has given a practical voice to an expanded view of what a course credit can look like. CBE formally recognizes that credit-worthy learning can happen outside formal institutions by tacitly recognizing that "school" is everywhere. Indeed, broadening our recognition of "course work" seems like the respectful thing to do. After all, if there are many ways to learn, and students can prove they have met the competencies for a course, then why shouldn't they get credit for the course? The only thing worse than not learning something you need to know is being forced to learn something you already know.

Institutions will increasingly find themselves in the brokering and evaluation business, being asked to validate student work that originated outside their institutions. This may make them feel uncomfortable because they won't have the direct experience with students they are used to having. Blended education is destined to mean not only blending media, or blending onsite and online venues, but also blending what we do at one school with what we do somewhere else, whether at a school or through other means.

The CBE approach will not be limited to higher education. It will increasingly be used in K-12, which until recently has been primarily a seller's market. In recent years we have seen some changes that are more consumer driven. Charter schools and online learning options have emerged, but they are limited. Some districts allow students to apply to attend schools outside their immediate jurisdictions. And there have always been private schools for the financially fortunate. But geographic inflexibility is still the rule of the day. Children must attend the local school; there is very little latitude for them to move outside of their districts. Imagine being forced to shop only at the department store closest to you and not having the option to go to one a few miles away—or having to apply to a review board to be able to do so—and you get the idea. That inflexibility, along with testing mania and a number of social factors, will push us to consider alternative ways of educating ourselves and our children.

In addition, assessment alternatives will drive educational change. Schools will find themselves in competition with emerging approaches to accreditation, like badges or micro-credentials. We will see the growth of shorter, "stackable" courses in response to professional development needs that rapidly evolve as knowledge and customized learning needs and opportunities rapidly evolve. Users may well generate these courses, which are blessed by an accrediting organization, a process that would disintermediate the need for gateway "scholars" to be in charge of all course development and consecration. This approach to coursework will form a symbiotic relationship with these new kinds of accreditation.

For now, new accreditation approaches may have a small footprint. The tipping point will come when employers or even universities, begin asking candidates to specify their badges and micro-credentials when applying for a job or admission to school. Or perhaps employers will skip badges and micro-credentials altogether and simply ask to see the ePortfolios that applicants have generated, which will probably be a product of the education they have received at U3W. The point is that alternatives to traditional education will give rise to alternative ways for employers to evaluate prospective employees. Employers who question the value of a standard education as an indication of a job candidate's viability will come to depend on those alternatives.

Allow me to address the issue that seems to be at the heart of the seismic jitters that traditional education feels about many of the new learning alternatives: a concern for quality, that elusive characteristic that everyone thinks they know when they see, but few can define.

To many in traditional education, quality seems under siege lately by new approaches to teaching and learning. Recently I told a higher education strategic planning group that I could summarize my thirty plus years in higher education innovation with the following phrase: quality vs. flexibility. Quality vs. flexibility. We all want quality, but we need to be flexible enough to meet the new generation of students where they are. We can't discriminate against them because of where they live, or their work schedules, or how they learn, or the collaborative mediascape they are used to, or the fact that they unconsciously live in two worlds at once. To adapt to the evolving learner landscape, our goal must become to infuse quality into a flexible approach to learning.

Unfortunately, we often assume that the status quo provides quality when sometimes all it really provides is the comfortable familiarity that comes with inertia. We prefer "the sure thing" to the mysterious world outside our comfort zone, regardless of the results that our current approaches produce, or regardless of the outcomes that might be achieved using new approaches. Changing our attitude requires some fearlessness and an inquiring mind to open the door to new ideas about what quality can look like. Above all, it requires an absolute focus on whether or not students are learning. If our students learn by using unconventional methods, but are engaged in demonstrable, quality learning, then any issue we have with new educational approaches is ours, not theirs.

The last implication about being mobile and connected that I want to mention has to do with transmedia. Transmedia typically refers to telling a story, promoting a brand or running a business using different kinds of media, across multiple media platforms and channels. This includes using everything from Twitter to Instagram to YouTube to RL. Most TV shows, as well as news and other entertainment ventures, are transmedia to some extent. In fact, much of what we experience in the mediasphere these days uses some kind of transmedia approach.

Transmedia has been adopted by the business world en masse, but not so much by the education world. As educators we need to ask ourselves, "How would we teach math, or a new language, or project based learning using a transmedia approach?" Bear in mind that transmedia is just the first stop in our evolution. Soon we will become what media consultant Monica Helms calls transmersive, which combines immersion, which I discussed earlier, with transmedia. The point here is that a serious disconnect exists between the mediascape that our students experience in and out of school. Students, and the rest of the world, embrace transmedia. Schools do not. Our goal should be to better coordinate those mediascapes.

As you can see, a good deal flows from the confluence of immersion and connectivity. And we have certainly not exhausted the topic. But let's move on.

Building Block 3: Shifting from Text to Media Collage

This shift is all about the move away from text centrism and toward a multimedia, transmedia form of expression. This shift is about "writing techxt" in an era of "now media" in which each new medium or media channel contributes to the continually evolving "media collage." Let's consider each of these terms.

The backstory behind the word "te(ch)xt" is simply this: Each technology that allows us to read and write also generates new kinds of text and new literacies that go with it. Tech generates techxt, which is just a contemporary application of the perspective "the medium is the message." If we are mindful and literate about what we want to communicate, then we design content differently for the smart phone than we do for the big screen. We frame photos differently for square Instagram images than for landscape display. We write using different voices, depending on whether we intend to publish on a blog or in a journal. This means we have to be able to write what I have come to call "now media." I distinguish new media from now media in the following way. New media has become a generic term referring to anything beyond print. Now media reflects the fact that media evolves quickly, creating new media forms which evolve slowly and often imperceptibly on a continuing basis. For centuries, now media was print. Today, now media consists of all those new media that appear unannounced, often with a jolt, which promise to yield to the next big thing, whatever it turns out to be.

Each new medium that emerges becomes part of the "media collage," which is best represented today by the webpage, a multi-media, transmedia presentation platform that is now our primary information resource for both reading and writing. We use it to coordinate traditional and emerging media in an integrated multi-dimensional approach to communication. Each new medium that emerges needs to be integrated into the overall media collage, and affects the entire ecosystem of the collage, thereby changing the nature of literacy needed to command the parts of the collage as well as the whole.

An historical note: The first web page I created in the early 1990s contained only text because that is all that was available. Look how far we have come. And the future is just getting started.

At issue here is the fact that our new media become invisible quickly. I will never forget arguing the need to address the disruptive nature of literacy with a colleague, who assured me that students who were in command of three Rs would have all of the literacy foundations they needed to enjoy a successful future. To bolster his point, he showed me a website that he felt skillfully argued his point. The site used diagrams, images, videos, interviews, text and many of the components of the media collage. The elements of the collage were woven together with a professional sense of design, aesthetics, integration and navigation. In short, what he showed me was a great example of everything we don't teach students how to create in a world dominated by the 3Rs. When I pointed this out to my friend I could see the look of astonishment emerge on his face. He hadn't noticed. This is not unusual. As McLuhan liked to say, fish are the last to become aware of the water. We are swimming in now media. They often arrive with great fanfare, but then we adapt to them quickly. Thereafter, they become invisible to us.

We should expect to see innovative developments that extend the media collage to our bodies and environments, that include motion, immersive reality, more sensory information and new media we can't even imagine yet. Our job is to figure out when a new medium has stabilized enough, and is widely read enough, that we need to teach it as a literacy. We are left to discern the fundamental literacy shifts that undergird emerging media so that we can adjust our approach to what it means to read and write. Let's spend some time here, because our need to write techxt is changing everything.

Expanding writing begins with including visuals as part of our daily language. Here's another new word for today, screasel, which is created by combining the words screen and easel. Screasels are where most of us go now to paint. I am not saying we shouldn't use traditional painting methods. And I'm not suggesting we get rid of any art forms that exist. All of them are important. However, the reality is that many of us turn to digital alternatives because they allow us to do something that heretofore we could not do: We can erase.

Have you ever tried to erase an oil painting? It's not easy. However, with the invention of Photoshop we can all set up an e-Easel, break out the digital paints and make as many mistakes as we want with impunity. Visual editing programs brought the concept of word processing to image editing, providing self-teaching tools that enabled anyone to pursue the aesthetic and visual literacies that schools didn't address, and which had once been only the domain of professionals. Tools like these became the metaphor for inclusion, and democratized a communication technology revolution that had been reserved for the very few.

Consider the woman in the picture. She is using two screasels at once: the laptop and the cell phone. You may look at that and say, "Big deal." But just remember that if you were walking through a park and saw this 20 years ago, you probably would have notified the police. This was truly odd behavior. Not anymore.

If the laptop and mobile phone are screasels one and two, then screasel three is the television and screasel four is the movie theater. Somewhere in the mix are the smart pad and the digital watch.

23

Screasels are absolutely everywhere and promise to evolve. They will be printed on sleeves and activated on ordinary hard surfaces. They will exist in the air, as we wave our hands in front of ourselves to create our next masterpiece. For many years, paper and writing utensils were the only ubiquitous media for creating content. Now they have a great deal of company.

Remember this: Literacy has always meant consuming and producing the media forms of the day, whatever they are. If you can read but you can't write, you are only half literate. This was as true a century ago as it is now. But today it means that we need to be able to write now media, as well as consume it critically. We have to be able to write "te(ch)xt," whatever that evolves to be. Image editing is just the beginning. Today we need to be able to write video, audio, infographics, whatever it is we consume. Tomorrow? Who knows. More importantly, we need to develop the skills to coordinate and integrate the elements of the media collage in ways that are aesthetic, articulate and navigable.

I am not suggesting that we all need to be accomplished in the use of all forms of media expression. School doesn't require students to become genius writers or mathematicians. Instead, each of us needs to understand media well enough to be able to deconstruct and interpret media messages so that we can respond to them in their own language. That is, we need to be able to use our understanding of media messages to create original, media-based communication. We don't need to be great media communicators, simply competent. If we find that we are overwhelmed with media expression choices, then perhaps each of us needs to develop a generalized sense of media-based literacy, while developing specialized abilities in the use of just a few of them. However we decide to approach this area of expression, each of us needs to be able to write media. If we can't, then we are illiterate.

I will tell you something that has always struck me as odd.

We require students to read great writers and then tell our students, "Try to write like them." We require our students to study the work of great mathematicians and tell them, "Try to compute like them." We require our students to use great web resources and watch great documentaries, but we don't say, "Try to create media like them." Why not?

For a long time we had an excuse for not having students write media: The gear needed to do so was too bulky, expensive and hard to use. But something happened about 10 or 20 years ago, depending upon how geeky you are, that made writing media–or writing techxt–possible: The media production capabilities that had been once reserved for professional mediasts showed up on our personal computers. Using our new tools to create media wasn't easy at first. Transferring video material from a video camera to a computer used to require a huge budget, a baseball bat and a shaman. Then suddenly everything changed. I will never forget the first time I booted up an early version of iMovie, plugged in my video camera and watched as a dialogue box appeared on my screen that read something like, "I see you have plugged in a video camera. Would you like to download its content?" I wept. The long struggle with the gear was coming to an end. Instead, I could focus on what I wanted to create rather than on getting the technology to work. Writing techxt was about to take off.

Our new tools not only allow us to make media, but also distribute it. Back in the day, in order to broadcast media we had to own a TV or radio station. Now we can buy a $200 camera, plug it into our home broadband network and be a TV station. We can now write and distribute the media forms of the day that were once reserved only for professional mediasts who had big budgets and preferential channel access, and we can do so cheaply and easily. Media literacy used to mean understanding how large mass media companies persuaded consumers. Now, as of writing techxt, media literacy also has come to mean becoming literate in using the language and skills of media expression, allowing us to become persuaders ourselves. To paraphrase media sage Marshall McLuhan, 'the medium became the message.' Because we can make media, we do. Making media is now part of our communication imperative. How we do so, and what we say, is up to us.

Consider all the media tools that are within the grasp of anyone with a reasonably powerful smart phone: video, images, animation, augmented reality, touch-based media and who-knows-what is coming down the pike. If we want to be literate, we have to be able to write those media forms to some extent, not just read them. Being able to write media has a very practical value. If we want to communicate in a global culture using a language that is at least somewhat universal, then we will probably turn to the language of design, pictures, movement and color. Yes, there are differences among cultures in terms of what certain elements of media and design mean. But we find a good deal of similarities too, many more than if we were trying to communicate using two different written and spoken languages.

However, the question still squarely before us is this: What is education's role in promoting art and design as a language, teaching new media literacy and helping students understand how to create articulate, professional media? The Common Core did not help us answer this question. When my teachers used to say, "Your homework today is," I assumed I would create something that looked like black squiggles on a white background–writing, in other words. Now, homework can look like anything you see on the Web. The science of being a good teacher requires knowing a number of technologies and methodologies, while the art requires knowing when to use which. In an era of now media, there is an evolving menu of options. If students need to demonstrate an understanding of gravity, we could require them to write a paragraph of explanation, as is most typically done today. Or, we could require them to create a movie of a falling object, which they annotate using a free online editing program in order to document the rate of acceleration. Or we could ask them to create a simple game that not only shows their understanding of gravity, but can also be used to teach basic gravitational concepts to others. Writing is no longer the default. It has become one of a number of paints on the pedagogical palette.

We need to cultivate a new attitude about literacy, because the technology we see today is only the tip of an ever-growing iceberg. We need to be prepared for the fact that every new media that emerges in our now media culture will need to be folded into the ever-expanding media collage. Writing techxt will evolve. It will become multisensory, holographic, more immersive and take on forms we can't imagine. We can count on students adopting now media much faster than school systems. We need to move forward knowing that we will need to be able to write, not just consume, all the new media that is coming our way if we want to be fully literate. To do so, we will need new planning models that can accommodate the many surprises that await us.

Building Block 4: Adopting Art as the 4ᵗʰ R

I have already mentioned this, but let me be very clear. The fundamental literacy that underlies the media communication revolution is art.

Unfortunately, we are running on old tapes about the role of art in our daily lives. To test my old tape theory, how would you respond if your child announced she wanted to be an artist? You would want to say, "How wonderful!" But deep inside you might be thinking, "Oh my god, please no. You'll starve. You'll be living in my basement until you're 50 waiting for the world to understand your work. You won't have a normal life. Will I ever have grandkids?"

We don't need to respond this way anymore. My friends who are artists have a great deal of interesting, well paying work. Many don't have degrees. In our visual and design-oriented culture, we all want a piece of their eye. We need them to represent us on the Web. What happens when we see clumsy design and graphics in the mediasphere? The same thing that happens when we read bad writing. We think, "That's unprofessional" and we click to go somewhere else, often unconsciously. We need artists. And to at least some extent, we need to become artists ourselves.

As I recall, we were all on the way to becoming artists in our youth. We entered school with a penchant to visually and tactilely represent our world, through drawings, finger paints, sand castles and sculptures made of bricolage. This kind of innovation is our natural state. However, we quickly learned from our educational institutions that words and numbers would dominate our literacy landscape, while visual representation would take a back seat. We shouldn't expect this to change anytime soon, given the high-stakes, 3Rs testing culture that we have created for ourselves that does not value visual literacy or Art the 4th R. Our students will live in two worlds: the testing world, which is dominated by the three Rs, and the real world, which encompasses many forms of art and media expression. Confusion, both ours and theirs, is understandable.

Please note that I am not talking about the arts in education, which of course I love. I am talking about art as a very practical literacy, which serves as a common language, much as letters and numbers serve as common languages that span all curriculum areas, and areas of human enterprise. Given that our students are going to use sound, images and other media elements as a generalized language, we should be interested in helping them do so with articulation and artistry. If the SATs had caught up with the times they would have included at least a digital drawing component by now. Of course, this would mean that we need to teach drawing as a mandatory literacy in school. We would have to open that door.

But don't take it from me. In the words of Martin Scorsese, "We have no choice but to treat all the moving images coming at us as a language." And according to George Lucas, "If people aren't taught the language of sound and images, shouldn't they be considered as illiterate as if they left college without the ability to read and write?" Anyway, don't get me started. I start ranting and my voice gets really squeaky.

A corollary of Art the 4th R is: Practice creatical thinking. The word "creatical" simply means combining creative and critical thinking into a single process. We need to stop pitting critical thinking against creative thinking. We need to fuse the two halves of our brain, and say forevermore there is no such thing as a creative act that doesn't benefit from critical thinking, and vice versa. Creatical thinking facilitates an approach to work flow that uses all of our abilities in an integrated fashion. It embodies the perceptual adjustment we need to make and the mindset we need to embrace to be able to adapt to the evolving demands of media expression and the increasingly complex problem solving landscape that modern life presents to us.

Creatical thinking extends far beyond the art world. It embraces a broader way of looking at life. Having students view the world through both a critical and a creative lens helps them not only solve problems but also see them. I like problem solving activities as much as the next educator, but they often assume that an authority figure has identified a problem and handed it off to others to figure out. We need to help students identify problems, and in order to do that they need to be able "to see" in ways often thought to be reserved just for artists. Being an artist is not just something we need to do. It is a way we need to live.

Another corollary of Art the 4th R is "follow the DAOW

of literacy." The DAOW brings together four foundational literacies of our day: oracy, art creation, writing and using digital tools. I see great examples of the DAOW, like Hans Rosling's *200 Countries, 200 Years, 4 Minutes.* In it, he "performs" a statistical analysis of the evolution of health and wealth in 200 nations over two centuries. He does so against an augmented reality background, so it appears that he is pointing at graphs in front of him. Watch it, and ask yourself, why isn't this a standard kind of activity for students? Math, research, oracy, writing, technology–they are all there. These are the kinds of activities that schools could do, and should embrace, that would most certainly engage, challenge and educate our students. A key aspect of Rosling's presentation is the way he gets math to move. We should teach math as movement. After all, it is the language we use to describe a world that is always in motion at many levels, from the subatomic to the mundane to the intergalactic. We are attracted to movement on a fundamental level, a point I will address in depth in my presentation *The Art of the Story.* Rosling's work is a good example of how to use our natural inclination toward movement and story to address research and academic content. Incidentally. Hans Rosling's *Gapminder* site will let you play with this kind of presentation.

While I'm at it, I am going to continue my rant with a little bit more about mathematics.

Math used to be all about solving for X. But today an important part of math deals with huge data sets, the kind that Facebook, Google and most online companies generate as a natural course of events. They read our email and watch our movements to build profiles about us in order to be more... responsive? Invasive? We will talk more about this in another presentation. For now we need to understand that the math used to make sense of the oceans of data we generate and swim in each day rules much of our experience online. Students need to understand how and why this happens. I have worked with middle school students to develop infographics and mathematical data visualizations to describe their personal networks so they can see how they are connected to "Big Data" in a very personal way. These are increasingly the kinds of mathematical representation models that students will need to be able to create in school, as well as beyond school. Often, math can be about combining art, problem solving and numerical representation. But we have to open a door.

If you would, allow me to vent about one more math issue. While I thank my high school math faculty for all of their hard work despite the attitude I brought to class each day, I must say that I have not used much of what they taught me beyond basic algebra and bits of geometry. I have had to teach myself most of the math that is truly useful to me in order to deal with real life challenges and opportunities, like buying a house, running a business, managing investments, grasping the meaning of questionnaires and understanding the math of retirement. I don't understand how I entered adulthood so devoid of applied math skills. My concern goes beyond issues of personal, generalized utility. If we want our students to be entrepreneurs, then let's give them the math to be entrepreneurs. They're not going to get these skills bisecting circles. Not every student wants to be a scientist. For many students, calculus won't be helpful. But statistics might, as would the math they need to understand infographics and all of those user surveys that bombard them whenever they go online. Let's open up a second strand of mathematics and let's call it entrepreneurial math. Okay, end of math rant.

Building Block 5: Valuing Writing, for Old and New Reasons

This seems counter intuitive, given the rise of the media collage. However, we need to value writing now more than ever. As an author of novels, scholarly articles and reports, I always see a place for great fiction, as well as clear expository writing. These are the genres in which traditional writing truly shines. However, good writing is important for another reason: Good media is based upon good writing. We don't really understand this in education because we aren't asking students to make very much media. If we were, we would discover how important writing is as a pathway to informed, articulate media.

I have helped students produce thousands of pieces of media–I stopped counting long ago. Early on I discovered that the single most important criterion that distinguished the good from the not-as-good media was simply this: The good media was based on good research and good writing. "If it ain't on the page, it ain't on the stage" comes to mind. And what's on the page needs to work.

The evolving importance of writing appears in other ways as well. Different media venues for expression have created the need for different approaches to writing, confirming that the medium is the message. A book allows for the broad expatiation of ideas and flowing text, while web and slideshow presentations do not. Yet, when new media forms arrive at first we often try, as McLuhan noted, to force the new media to do the work of the old. That is, we try to squeeze the content of the previous medium into the new medium that is replacing it or competing with it. Eventually, after much experimentation, we discover that new media offer and even demand new kinds of expression.

Here is just one example of an expanded notion of writing, created by the abbreviated reading venues that populate the web. On the left we are looking at information in traditional form. On the right we are looking at the same information presented as VDT. No, VDT is neither a disease nor an undergarment brand. It stands for "visually differentiated text." It uses the 7 Bs: Breaks, Boldface, Bullets,

Value Writing

Essay form & **VDT form**

Banners, Boxes, Beyond black and white (color) and Beginnings, that is, providing the first part of a text presentation, then providing a link to the rest of it. Squint, and you can almost see it as a structured series of tweets.

The VDT approach to rhetoric provides more visual toeholds. It provides ways to scan information so readers can orient themselves quickly to material they are reading in order to decide whether or not they want to invest their time in a particular text presentation. VDT is just one response to our need for tools to process the overwhelming amount of information in our lives. Should we teach students how to use this as one approach to writing? In an era of massive info inundation, absolutely. The goal of VDT is to provide clear, easily accessible, informed communication for the digitally deluged information consumer.

As we upgrade our approach to literacy, we also need to stop thinking about it as a purely personal pursuit. I remember being tested for literacy as a child. Doctor somebody in a bowtie would visit our class to administer a literacy exam. Weeks later, the school would call our parents and tell them how literate we were.

Individualized literacy testing is still with us, of course. In fact, it dominates education. But there is more to literacy these days. I see many students picking up our slack, teaching themselves and each other media, visual, collaborative and other literacies that writing techxt demands, because we don't teach these at school. We do not test for these literacies, so they are not in the curriculum. The ability to "write a wiki" or a web page with a team, practice netiquette and effective communication within an online environment, or develop a piece of cooperative media–all of these skills fall under the heading of social literacy and are largely ignored. Because testing drives so much of education these days, and testing is focused on personal literacy and not social literacy, I don't expect this to change anytime soon.

Building Block 6: Seeing Through a Digital Citizenship Lens

This building block addresses the ethical literacies and perspectives needed to successfully manage a digital lifestyle. Our goals for ourselves and our students are as follows: be safe, ethical and responsible; be inspired, innovative and involved; be passionate, reflective and empathetic; be informed, savvy and ultimately wise; be a researcher, participant and leader. I address this area of inquiry in detail in my book, *Digital Community, Digital Citizen,* as well as in another presentation in this series. Here I want to explore it briefly so we understand the scope it embraces.

Digital citizenship covers an area that is both broad and deep. Most of us experience it as a list of issues that terrify and threaten us: sexting, cyberbullying, Internet stalking, acting inappropriately online and so on. To be sure, these are real issues that need to be understood and addressed. But the real revolution in digital citizenship needs to come in terms of how we frame our entire educational experience, from mission statement to curriculum. Currently we bob and weave every time a new technology emerges that invents a new behavior that vexes us. Treating digital citizenship solely as a list of issues is exhausting and ineffective, and won't help us build the foundation that we need as we head into a future of unparalleled innovation that is just getting started.

We need to place digital citizenship within a broader ethical framework that is both theoretical and practical. For this reason I feel quite certain that at some point we will wish we had created a character education program as a foundation for our digital citizenship efforts.

To help us understand this, let's imagine that a school board somewhere shares this view. It might produce a mission statement like this: "Students will study the personal, social and environmental impacts of every technology and media application they use in school." To me, this is just a beginning point. Students should also be looking at emerging technologies that will affect them beyond school. But we'll start here.

This mission statement seems harmless enough. However, good luck finding something like it in use today. I find snippets of the sentiment it embodies here and there. Overall, however, this perspective is simply not on the table. We are not cultivating this type of big picture perspective with our students and school communities.

How we address digital citizenship really depends on what kind of people we want our students to become. What do I want for our children? I want them to be passionate about their learning, but I also want them to be reflective about their passions. I want students to engage, but I also want them to disengage for the purpose of taking stock of their lives and placing their activities, technologies and goals in a larger perspective. I want their pursuits to be driven by community interest and personal transformation, rather than simply propelled by the need to achieve.

Practically speaking, I want students to understand that connective and disconnective properties are embedded in all technologies. I want them to be able to see both and strike a balance between them as they forge their individual interpretations of living a digital lifestyle. They will need this skill in order to navigate and shape a world in which innovation will continue to move like a roller coaster without a braking system, and never slow down. We see examples of "connect-disconnect" everywhere. My cell phone connects me easily to people far away, while disconnecting me from the people sitting right next to me. All of my transportation technologies do something similar by encouraging me to form networks with people who are not in my immediate, geographic neighborhood. A quick scan of tech news recently yielded stories about self-driving cars involved in accidents, neurological "thinking caps" that can improve our cognition and robots that can reproduce themselves. Each of these embodies profound connections and disconnections. Technologies like these represent the future our students are inhabiting and will have a hand in creating. And the future is just getting started. It's best to start thinking about connections and disconnections now.

I also want our students to be historians and futurists. I want them to understand that the great, unfolding pageantry of innovation can largely be understood in terms of what Dertouzos called "the ancient human" within each of us. As head of MIT Computer Science for many years, Dertouzos wrote eloquently about how to predict the success of technology not based on its newness, but rather on its appeal to longstanding human needs. Consider Facebook through Dertouzos' lens. On the one hand, it seems new and exciting. All of those megabits flying through the air and landing on someone else's smart phone half a world away seems truly modern. This certainly wasn't part of my grandparents' experience. On the other hand, using Facebook seems to be just the latest way to do things that the essential, ancient human in all of us has craved to do all along: form community, maintain the bonds of family and friends, and share stories. Prior to Facebook, I expected to see extended family members once every few years, largely depending on happenstance. Now I share information and stories with them frequently in the great electronic commons. The bottom line here is that we tend to see social media as new, rather than as new responses to very old needs. This perspective will help students become more insightful futurists and, if we're lucky, more informed and active nowists.

In addition, I want our students to develop a more informed relationship with the information they consume. On one level this means developing the abilities needed to find trustworthy information sources. On a deeper level, it involves developing a savvy, sixth sense about the motives behind those who produce the information they consume. Often, we are being pitched rather than presented information. The difference between the two approaches is often extremely subtle. We need to see the agenda behind the screen. As Steve Goodman, Director of the Educational Video Center, succinctly put it, "Media is a filter while pretending to be a clear window." We need to give students the media literacy skills they need to distinguish the filter from the window.

On a still deeper level, we need students to understand that the most poignant filters they bring to information gathering are their own biases. This cuts both ways. On the one hand, we want them to follow their passions, an approach to life that constitutes a kind of bias. On the other hand, we want them to know that at the core of the human condition is the fact that we filter information through our biases, shading and distorting the information we receive in the process. Because of this, we often make up our minds before we acquire information, not afterwards. For example, when listening to particular politicians we don't like, we tend to find reasons to disagree with what they are saying, or we hear what we want to hear in their words, regardless of what they intend, or regardless of the facts they bring to the table. We apply this kind of perceptual myopia to those we are predisposed to agree with as well. And we apply it to most situations we encounter, whether they involve friends,

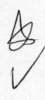

people in the news or the results of an information search. One of the most important information literacy skills our students can develop is the ability to understand their own biases, so they can distinguish between what they are actually observing and what they think they are seeing. We need to burn this into our psyches: Everything touched by us contains our bias.

However, when do any of us have an opportunity to think and talk about these issues? Where are issues like these in the curriculum? As we head over the high-stakes testing cliff, I'm afraid these truly important issues are rarely addressed. I am also afraid that they will be addressed only if school systems frame the educational experience in ways that value the big picture perspective that is offered by digital citizenship. One of the most useful skills we could help students develop is the ability to assess the impacts of technology and the Internet, on themselves, their communities, the world and the environment. Unfortunately, such a focus is rare.

There are better ways to proceed. If I could change one aspect of our approach to digital citizenship in schools, it would be to stop having adults make all the Internet rules for students. When we don't involve students in rule making, we rob them of the opportunities they need to develop their ethical muscles. Remember this: If students don't frame the system, then they game the system. And we want them framing the system. This only comes through practice.

To provide students an opportunity to practice, I engage them in an activity called *You're In Charge*. They are tasked with developing policies about how technology can be used in school, and what should happen when students misuse their privileges. They tackle a range of issues, from the digital manipulation of photos, to cyberbullying, to what students should be able to publish online in the form of ePortfolios. And I pitch them new technologies to grapple with, like iGlasses that are connected to the Internet, and robot assistants they might bring to school one day. I ask them, "Should we have them at school? Under what conditions?" The results are amazing. They almost instantly cultivate a more adult attitude about their digital lifestyles. They often become quite conservative in their outlooks and behavioral expectations. We mistakenly suppose that students can't think clearly about how to manage these situations because they are too immature or cognitively challenged. My experience suggests that in many cases the real reason that we don't see evidence of their abilities in this area is because we don't give them opportunities to use them. By not involving them, we deprive them of opportunities to practice their ethical reasoning skills, as well as to take advantage of our guidance as they navigate morally ambiguous territory. I assure you they need our guidance. I will never forget the time a group of 8th graders with whom I was working proposed that anyone being mean on the Internet should spend a night in jail, starting with 3rd graders. Our students do need us.

Of particular importance is the issue of developing a positive digital footprint, which I think is probably the only recourse we have to counter being overwhelmed by the Web and by other people's portrayal of our identity in the infosphere. Unless we plan on using obscure screen names, we're not going to be able to hide anymore. This means that we had better present ourselves in ways that we want others to see. We have all heard the horror stories. Someone snaps a picture of you at a party with a lampshade on your head, posts it on Facebook, and suddenly potential employers stop returning your calls. This is the new normal and we need to help students deal with it.

However, alongside striking a defensive posture we also need to take a more positive approach. Each of us needs to deliberately manage our online identity. In practical terms this means creating some kind of ePortfolio or web presence that we show to the world that is thoughtful, articulate, professional and authentic. The reality is that if we don't tell our story, others will do it for us, and few of us would be happy with the results. We need to help students tell their stories to the world that represent their accomplishments and best intentions.

An ePortfolio provides a great opportunity for us to take stock. If we don't have much to put on our ePortfolios, then we have important questions to consider: What are we doing with our lives? What do we wish we were doing? What and who do we want to be when we grow up? These are all great questions to ask at any age.

However, when do we talk about what an ePortfolio is and what the life behind it might look like? When do we talk about all the life-changing technologies that swirl around us like air? Do we talk about them in school? I don't see it very often. Do 13-year-olds naturally gather and ask themselves, "I wonder how the nature of immersive reality is changing our essential humanity?" Probably not. Do you talk about it at home with your kids? I hope so. Maybe at church? I don't know. The bottom line is that we don't talk about the things that are really changing us. It is a conversation we need to have. But in order to make room for such a conversation, we would need to open a very big door.

Building Block 7: Harnessing Story

I go into this in great detail in the presentation, *The Art of the Story.* Here I will provide a brief overview.

We don't value storytelling in education because we see it as entertainment. Fluff. The opposite of academic rigor. But it is so much more than that.

Stories are highly efficient information containers that are much more engaging than the other major information container we use: the list. The reason for this is simple: Stories provide information in an interrelated, integrated context, while lists often do not. Without context, we experience chaos.

We naturally seek to connect the dots in our world, and that usually means creating some kind of narrative to go along with whatever we experience. The business world understands this. The media world knows this. But education is slow to pick up on it.

Kiernan Egan wrote an insightful book called *Teaching as Storytelling.* In it he made the following point: By the time children start school they already have been immersed in the story form. They have experienced it through comics, TV shows, conversations, books read to them by their parents, conversations around the dinner table and a number of other sources. However, at school they often encounter information in list form. The mixing of the two information forms creates a kind of cognitive and emotional dissonance. Often, when students tell us that they are bored or that school material is too difficult, they are really saying, "Where's the story?" For a number of emotional, neurological and perhaps survival-based reasons, stories are part of our psyche. Yet we don't tap into that foundation of the human condition very well in school.

Besides being efficient, stories are also emotionally engaging, an attribute we don't often associate with textbooks or reports. Come to think of it, I have never heard anyone tell me that they liked to read reports, or seen anyone identify "likes reading reports" as a personal attribute on Facebook. If you saw that, would you friend that person? Reports are important and we read them, but they rarely move us. A well-told story, on the other hand, can change the world.

As a storyteller, I am primarily associated with the digital storytelling field. However, I spend most of my time in the storytelling world teaching about the nature of story, regardless of how a story is going to be expressed. The technology used to tell a media-based story is important but secondary. A weak story amplified by technology is painful to watch. When I work with students and clients, I spend much of my time helping them understand what a story is and how it works. I have developed story planning tools that have proven to be helpful in this regard, which I cover in detail in a later presentation. Here I just want to tell you about the heart of my process: the story core.

The story core consists of three elements: problem, transformation, resolution; not beginning, middle and end, as most have been taught. In a sentence, an effective story is one in which people solve problems, overcome obstacles and change in the process. Of course, stories are typically much more detailed. However, without a solid core the details don't matter. You will find the story core in nearly every movie, novel, commercial campaign, ad or documentary that engages you. When I help others frame their messages, I spend most of my time on the core. Once that is in place, the details are theirs. The story core is highly adaptable to units of instruction and other educational endeavors. The story core in education is basically the same, but the three points of the story core often become inquiry, discovery and learning. I use the story core for all of my storytelling activities: fiction writing, voice-over narration, green screen performance, course development, and even music composition. The story core is universal and quintessentially human.

Let me tell you about a story that shows the story core in action. It is a math story. I like to show math stories in order to shake people out of their belief that stories can only be used in language arts and history projects. The story as an "information container" can be used for any subject area, commercial enterprise or personal pursuit.

How to Animate a Rolling Ball was created a number of years ago by Glen Bledsoe's fourth grade class. In this video, students use animation software to make a ball roll across a beach. Their first attempt doesn't work—the ball skids instead of rolls across the sand. Not only is this physically very unlikely

42

to happen, it also looks odd and unnatural. The students regroup, learn some more math, and try again. In the process they explain the math equations they use and why. Their second attempt succeeds!

What turned this media piece from a report into a story? After all, the students could have simply presented the math of a rolling ball successfully: Here's the ball, here's how it rolls and here's the math behind it. Assignment done. The reality is that had they used this approach, the audience would have forgotten about their story quickly. What turned their work into a memorable story? This fact: There was a problem, which is a kick-starter for most stories and a point of entry for viewers. There was also a transformation, as the students learned new math, and explained how they applied it. And finally there was resolution, as the ball finally rolled. They successfully included the three points of the story core and, as a result, engaged us as an audience.

The introduction of a problem into the narrative is the hook. A problem is the most essential of the story core's three legs because it gets the ball rolling, so to speak. When the ball skidded instead of rolled across the sand, each one of us in our own way wondered, "What are they going to do about that?" We leaned forward in our chairs, wanting to know what was going to happen next. We became emotionally invested in the information set, and how events were going to unfold. That's how story works. Note that the students' learning process looks a good deal more like real life and real learning, because we see a failed attempt on the way to success. Also notice how their process stands in complete contrast to simply getting and presenting the right answer. When we focus on how students learn, and require them to document their process, we gain a portal into who they are and how they learn. We turn education from a report into a story.

Two comments about storytelling and personal growth.

First, beyond the academic applications of story, students will find great value in developing personal stories. People live within their stories. They often get stuck there. Their stories can be about feeling misunderstood or frustrated, or about having goals that they don't know how to express. The only way for them to change their stories is to tell them. Once they hear them aloud, whether spoken or through digital means, they can actually begin to think about how to alter them.

Students who develop ePortfolios as a way of taking stock of and documenting their accomplishments and dreams can see their stories unfold, and actively engage in the process of changing them. Developing ePortfolios is a great way for them to become heroes of their own life stories. As I mentioned earlier, students need to be in command of their own stories. If they aren't, then others will control their stories, and no one wants that. Because we are witnesses to their unfolding stories, we can provide perspective and guidance, not just about their academic growth, but also their dreams and aspirations. Incidentally, I have often found that it is quite difficult for many students to see all of the interesting and wonderful things they do, a fact that is at once both fascinating and disheartening. They need our help to zoom out, and see their lives in a much broader and richer perspective. We need to open that door.

Second, the greatest leaders and communicators are also great storytellers. If we are wondering what to include in our wish list of student outcomes, one item should most definitely be the ability to tell an effective, engaging story. Students can do this in traditional, stand-and-deliver fashion, in a more mediated fashion or both. What's important to understand is that having the ability to convey important information in narrative form is critical to engaging their professional, educational and personal communities. But, we don't test for this ability. So, I fear this will receive very little attention.

44

Building Block 8: We'll See...

I always try to leave it open. When it gets here, I'll let you know. Whatever it is, it'll be big.

However I will say this. Making stuff is now a literacy. It always has been, but it is finally receiving the attention it deserves, largely through efforts like "the maker movement," which is dedicated to solving real world engineering problems by inventing and creating real things using materials in physical space. We need to provide spaces for invention, engineering and making things. Those of you in education are quite familiar with the acronym STEM–or STEAM, which adds Art to Science, Technology, Engineering and Math. The STEAM and maker movements will form a symbiotic relationship because they need each other to flourish. New technological advancements, like those in 3D printing and the Internet of Things, will cause maker spaces and media spaces to merge. After all, the "things" in our lives are often driven by software, and interface with the larger digital domain of the Web. We are currently watching the maker movement embrace coding, largely as a way to control hardware. Perhaps at the intersection of these two worlds, math will really begin to move. Perhaps making stuff is where the actual and the digital really combine and take off. Perhaps making stuff is building block number eight, and I will simply have to add building block number nine when it emerges. Of course, then I would need to give longer presentations. Stay tuned.

Let me close with some advice.

The first piece of advice has to do with techies vs. teachies. It is advice that is easily applicable to any work environment in which IT is in command of the communication infrastructure.

One time I was making a presentation about this topic in which I was talking about how to address the fact that teachies and techies often had a hard time communicating. Afterwards, a group of teachers approached me to tell me how much they adored their IT director. He was in the audience and they offered to introduce us. I was delighted.

I asked him what he did that generated so much love and he was very specific. Two things from that conversation stuck out. First, he offered to go to any faculty or curriculum meeting that would have him. That way when ideas came up that involved IT, he could help find solutions on the spot. This wasn't typical by any means. Traditionally, an academic department would come up with an idea, chase down the IT folks, and at the next month's meeting announce, "I asked IT about our idea and they said no." There may be many reasons why this dynamic is so prevalent, but at the heart of all of them is a lack of direct communication. To address this situation the IT director changed the communication culture. He came to faculty meetings, hammered out compromises and helped teachers move forward, as quickly and as painlessly as possible. His approach kept the wheels of innovation turning.

By the way, I will pass on some advice that has served me well over the years. Find the time to walk into your IT office, cookies in hand, and announce that you don't need a thing, and dropped by just to thank everyone for keeping everything working. Think about it. Most of the calls that IT professionals receive are from people stressed and screaming about the fact that their printers weren't working an hour before a grant needed to be submitted. When you show up not wanting a thing, in a good mood and grateful for their work, you are a slice of heaven. Do you know what this approach has gotten me over the years? Anything I wanted. I watched many times as my work order magically floated to the top of the IT in-basket. IT folks are human beings. Treat them as such and watch what happens.

The second point I recall from the conversation with the adored IT director was that he required each of his employees to "get up from the bench" and visit a classroom for at least half an hour each week. He said it was how he kept his employees grounded and reminded them who the real clients were. He said it worked wonders.

The second piece of advice I have to offer has to do with what teachers want from administrators. I call it the CARES system: Compensation, Assistance, Recognition, Extra time and Support for risk taking. Even though all of these are important, when I drill down I find that the element of the CARES system that teachers really want, and can't get any other way, is the last of these: support from administrators for taking a risk with a new idea or program. It is the one element of the CARES system for which they can't compensate by using their own time or their own money, no matter how generous they are. Taking risks requires those in charge to open the door.

If a teacher has a great idea to use a wiki in biology or YouTube in social studies, often she needs an administrator to flip a switch to allow access to those kinds of services. Teachers can't do that on their own–they aren't the gatekeepers. If you're an administrator, be an activist administrator. Find your innovators and ask them what doors they need you to open. I'm not saying you need to open the door for everybody all at once, but at least go find that 10% to 15% of the teachers who are ready to try out some great ideas, and open the door for them. Then, when they prove themselves, you're going to want to open that door for others. Expand slowly if you must, but keep expanding. Again, I encourage you to see how you can apply this to literally any modern workplace. The desire to innovate is all around you, but is often frustrated by a lack of recognition and opportunity. Innovators need door openers.

And finally, my third piece of advice: Turn concerns into goals.

How often have we experienced something like this? A group of teachers have a great idea. They're going to require students to use Wikipedia, the National Archives and Records

Administration database and the National Science Foundation website as resources for the creation of documentaries about local issues based on research conducted with students around the world. Maybe they are studying climate change, or local customs, or are cooperatively designing a robot. Then, they are going to create a documentary that they post on YouTube for the entire world to see. It will become part of a student-based video library, called *How Students See the World.*

Seven out of eight of the teachers in the group are excited and can't wait to get started. But then there's Dana. Please note that I am using a gender-neutral name. If your name is Dana, I'm not picking on you. Pretend I'm talking about Kim, also a gender-neutral name. I'll let you sort it out.

Back to our educators. In the middle of the meeting, at the apex of enthusiasm, Dana announces, "I have concerns." You know what happens, don't you? Forward motion stops as everyone workshops the insecurities of a group member. No one wants to be insensitive! All too often, the project simply grinds to a halt. All too often in situations like these we miss a critical perspective: A concern is just a negatively stated goal. That's all it is. So, you need to turn the situation around by transforming the concern into a goal.

Rather than give up, ask the question, "Dana, what's your concern?" Dana might say something like, "I'm concerned that students aren't going to write enough because they're doing all this media stuff." I hear that now and again. Your response should be: "Great, we have a new goal. Dana, we're going to use your rubric for writing, and we're going to fold that into the project. Also, we are going to require a report that is five pages long? No? Six pages? Are you good? Are we set?" Then vote. It may be seven to one, but at least you don't keep your students from getting the education they deserve. Changing concerns into goals is a universal strategy, adaptable to many environments and situations.

My last piece of advice is exemplified by that road sign. I love that sign. Notice it doesn't say "Slow down," it says "Good luck!" And that is what I wish to say to you: Don't slow down, and good luck.

And whatever you do, please go tell your story.

Thank you.

DIGITAL CITIZENSHIP

Ethics During Times of Extreme Change

I am declaring the next hour a fear-free zone.

For the next hour, I want you to suspend your fears about the Internet and social media. Instead, I want you to focus on placing your digital lifestyle in a larger perspective. I want you to embrace the goal of striking a balance between outrageous opportunity and informed awareness; between passionate engagement and reflective action; between being absorbed at the keyboard and stepping back from the screen. Achieving this balance lies at the heart of dancing gracefully and purposefully with digital change. And fear will not help us dance.

Unfortunately, fear is what I often encounter whenever I bring up the topic of digital citizenship. I can really buzz kill a party that way. I certainly don't mean to. I want audiences to engage just as enthusiastically as they do when I regale them with tales of new media in education, or digital storytelling in mental health, or media psychology in business and branding. But the reality is that any serious consideration of digital citizenship tends to breed a quiet panic, and fill audience's minds with visions of cyberbulliers and online predators. To many, it raises the specter of the digital revolution's dark side, which is as vast and unfathomable as it is troublesome and threatening.

To counter this attitude, those of us in the digital citizenship world should embrace two goals. The first is to figure out how to make digital citizenship fun and interesting, something I don't see very often. As my grandmother used to say, "A task that is fun is already half done." I will introduce some activities toward the end of this presentation that should help address that objective.

The second goal is to portray digital citizenship for what it is: the most positive development in education since the Internet became a fixture in our lives. Digital citizenship provides a real opportunity to rebuild our educational systems. It gives us the chance we have been waiting for to develop approaches to education that reflect the ethical and innovative perspectives we cherish, and to build the futures we want for ourselves and our children. However, we need to suspend our fear in order to be able to think in terms of these possibilities.

Getting Situated–What Is Digital Citizenship?

For now, let's get situated. What is digital citizenship? Generally speaking, it is the umbrella term that many use to address a broad area of inquiry and activity related to the ethics, concerns and opportunities associated with living a digital lifestyle. As I mentioned in an earlier presentation, in education digital citizenship reflects our quest to help students, as well as ourselves, develop the skills and perspectives necessary to live a digital lifestyle that is safe, ethical and responsible; inspired, innovative and involved; passionate, reflective and empathetic; informed, savvy and ultimately wise. We want all students to be able to assume the roles of researcher, participant and leader as they build communities that effectively span their real and online worlds.

By a "digital lifestyle" I mean a socially mediated, technologically infused, mobile lifestyle that implies many new considerations for citizenship that were not in play during earlier times. One of these considerations is that we live a very empowered lifestyle. We, as individuals and as groups, can push a few buttons and exert immense influence on the few and the many, near and far away. Another consideration is that our new lifestyles are both invisible and omnipresent. On the one hand, they are subterranean, allowing us to travel the passageways of the Internet out of public view if we wish. On the other, they are also very public. We can broadcast what we do to millions, intentionally or without even noticing, leaving behind our digital footprints wherever we go.

The quality that makes our new lifestyle truly unique is one I explored in an earlier presentation, namely, that we now live in two places at once. We live in real life (RL), as well as in immersive reality (IR), the world on the other end of our smart devices, which are, to quote, MIT's Sherry Turkle, "always on, and always on us." The media ecologists see us as occupying two ecosystems, our natural ecosystem and what I call our "tEcosystem" (pronounced TEE-co-system), a world of real time media that travels with us wherever we go. Our two ecosystems are similar in that they consist of global, interdependent systems and subsystems that are nearly impossible to disentangle, and which can only be understood holistically within the context of the entire network. The main difference between them is that our primary ecosystem degrades very slowly, while our secondary tEcosystem can fail quickly and pervasively.

Whatever we call our two worlds, it can be quite challenging to reconcile them and navigate the multi-dimensional reality they create. As a character in my novel, *Then What?,* says about this phenomenon, "There's where's your mind, and there's where's your behind, and sometimes the two just don't align." We are all trying to manage and integrate our online and offline selves as the future rapidly unfolds in unforeseen ways. If you are a parent, you are looking over your children's shoulders wondering what they are doing online and worrying about their safety in RL and IR. If you are concerned about yourself, then you are looking over your own shoulder wondering who is watching you and what they will do with the information they find.

Let's talk a bit about our second world, which I call the land of partycipation, pronounced just like "participation." I gave it that name because being online is like being at a big party. Actually, it is more like being at a Mardi Gras of the mind, with many special attributes and party favors not typically found at other gala events. At partycipation there are millions of attendees, with more joining daily. It costs very little to attend, and we can join from just about anywhere. We meet new people, make new friends, forge alliances, conduct business—whatever our encounters call for. Partycipation allows us to have multiple identities, as well as to experiment with our persona as new social situations emerge. We are free to identify ourselves or we can opt to use the masquerade option to shield our true identities. We can be whoever we want and say basically whatever we want, to whomever we want about whatever we want. This also means that we never really know with whom we are communicating, or whether what they say is remotely true.

At partycipation, we have access to an ever-expanding cornucopia of resources that are dreamlike in scope and variety. We can literally think about something, search for it, and find it: classic movies, old classmates, interactive recipes, Tweet feeds about poodle grooming, augmented reality tattoos, you name it. Only our imaginations limit what we can find and do. We can take home a copy of much of what we see and hear, knowing that the owner will not lose his original, copyright issues aside for the moment. We can even modify whatever we find and give it back to the party as something borrowed but "ouriginalized."

But, wait — there's more! If all of this weren't enough to entice us to join, partycipation does not require a dress code, and does not produce any negative health effects, except those associated with sitting too long, as well as some psychological issues that are surfacing about our over-involvement in the online world. Amazingly, we experience this unbelievable bounty within a kind of emotional myopia that allows us to feel only passing concerns about any sense of injury or repercussion to ourselves or others. Given this much freedom, at this little cost, ethical issues were bound to emerge.

Regardless of how you feel about life at the great electronic gathering, our current interest in digital citizenship is driven by the fact that many of our children attend this party. We are also concerned that partycipation can be used as a gateway to real life and vice versa. The interplay between the two worlds can be anything from complimentary to contradictory, from a direct way of reinforcing an integrated view of identity, to an indirect means of circumventing public attention in order to pursue separate presentations of self. Regardless of how we use our online venues, we need to be concerned because as Turkle reminds us, "the job of adolescence is centered around experimentation—with ideas, with people, with notions of self." Prior to the infosphere, adults could witness the identity play and development of maturing youth and intervene when necessary. But the invisible world of personal networks has made this much more difficult.

Above all, we shouldn't lose sight of how significant partycipation is in the evolution of human events. We are basically reinventing society through our "now media" in terms of the new ways that we define and present ourselves, and interact with others, as well as how we create and share ideas and content. In many ways, the Internet presents us with the absolute freedom that the existentialists have been telling us has always been our birthright and natural state. We are free to create human nature as we see fit by virtue of the choices we make. In the process, we establish norms, values and a sense of personal and collective identity. How we interpret this freedom opens up a window into the human condition and the nature of the human psyche that is historically unparalleled in terms of depth, scope and intrigue. As we develop this new area of human endeavor in our own image, we produce an extreme edge of freedom that causes us our greatest concerns.

Remember this: While we might talk a good game about goals, ethics and the greater good, partycipation reminds us that we are what we do. We can respond to the overwhelming freedom we are presented in our online world as seriously or lightly, as altruistically or selfishly, and as virtuously or nefariously as we wish. We can reinvent the world according to our "better angels," or we can squander this opportunity by creating mountains of drivel and worlds of hurt. We can build connections or disconnections. It is up to us.

Okay, there I go, bringing down the mood of the room again. So let me rebound by saying that digital citizenship offers tremendous opportunities to reinvent ourselves personally, educationally and culturally. I am here to talk to you about how that can happen and why digital citizenship is something we need to be addressing in schools at all levels, K through PhD, as well as in our personal and professional lives, regardless of what we do for a living. I am going to make the case that digital citizenship is the lens through which we need to view the world if we want to safeguard its future and our quality of life, as well as take advantage of the best that our innovative selves have to offer. But first, let me set the stage by providing a bit of history and context about digital citizenship that I think you will find helpful.

A Brief History of Digital Citizenship

The technological sphere only became concerned with citizenship when the Internet was created and led to the development of common virtual space. This led to the formation of communities, which in turn made us wonder what it meant to belong to those communities, and what our expectations of each other were as community members. Citizenship has always been associated with the rights and responsibilities of living in a community. This has not changed over the centuries. However, now we are also citizens of a new second reality that qualifies as a community: an immersive, online reality. As we go forward, digital citizenship is the overarching term and perspective that attempts to capture our concerns about living in that second reality, as well as blending our lives online and in real life into one integrated, healthy approach to living. This is what we want for our children, our societies and ourselves.

Digital citizenship also includes some legacy concerns about technology and society that preceded the World Wide Web. Prior to the advent of the Internet, these concerns were given the broad umbrella term, "the social impacts of technology." In its original set of educational technology standards, ISTE (International Society for Technology in Education) described this area as "social, ethical and human issues."

Let me tell you how my concern for the social impacts of technology played out in my life as an educator. During the early 1980s, while I was teaching at the University of Alaska Southeast, I helped to create one of the very early educational technology master's degrees in direct response to Apple IIe computers and three hundred baud modems. For the youngsters in the audience, the Apple IIe was the first personal computer to be both useful and lovable. A modem was a device that allowed us to connect our personal computers to a mainframe via the telephone system, creating rudimentary social media opportunities well in advance of the Internet. The term "baud" refers to the transmission speed that a modem supported. And three hundred baud modems were very, very slow.

Excuse me as I wax historically for a moment: Those of you who came of age during the broadband era have never really experienced slow. Three hundred baud was so slow that you could hear each letter land on the screen with an audible "thunk." My colleagues and I would crowd around one of those huge CRT computer monitors with fuzzy, headache-inducing resolution in order to read an arriving email. We would watch with great anticipation as the letters slowly crawled across the screen. After a few characters appeared, we'd start betting on what the word was going to be. We had plenty of time to consider our options.

In retrospect, that old technology provided a good lesson about the fact that disruptive innovation is ultimately contextual. As slow and cumbersome as the system was, we changed the lives of remote correspondence students who had no access to school by giving them the earliest laptops available. The laptops allowed them to send and receive homework much faster than by mail, which often arrived from the interior of Alaska via floatplane and dog sled. The result was that students experienced a much more responsive educational experience than they had been used to, in some cases reducing turnaround time for homework from six weeks to six hours. Those laptops, with their three hundred baud modems, significantly disrupted the status quo of rural education. But enough reminiscing.

As I was saying, I was part of a team that helped develop an early master's degree in educational technology. One of our primary goals for the program was to offer students a balanced perspective of technology, which included course work that considered the downside of technology, or at least looked at technology in objective, balanced terms. As the digital revolution zoomed off, everyone seemed to be in "go" mode, rather than "let's pause and think this through" mode. There was a good deal of conversation about what technology could do for us, but very little discussion about what it could do to us. Along with wanting our students to enjoy all the excitement in the air about using the new tools, we also wanted them to consider the "social, ethical and human issues" associated with living a technological lifestyle. We wanted to educate the whole person.

In a course I offered for many years, named *The Social Impacts of Technology,* we looked at how technology impacted our cultures and our social and interpersonal relationships, as well as our relationships with the environment and ourselves. We considered a wide range of issues, from the resocializing nature of refrigeration, to the psychology of TV advertising, to the democratization of writing caused by the advent of word processing. Then, when the Internet came along, going online became the disruptive addition to all of this, as did going mobile years later. Two characteristics drove the disruption. First, these developments were inherently connective and socializing, building communities where there were none before; stand-alone technology simply did not do this nearly as effectively. Second, the new technology turned us from consumers, who studied the impacts of technology, into participators who created the impacts. The result was that the social impacts of technology morphed into digital citizenship. Unfortunately, I think digital citizenship is a bit heavy on cyber considerations, often at the expense of focusing on the earlier, legacy considerations about living a technological lifestyle, which are still very relevant. But that's another topic.

Incidentally, the final assignment in the *Social Impacts of Technology* course was to write a letter from the future. Students had to pitch themselves twenty years into the future and report back about what they saw and how it came to be. Every letter students created was a fascinating read. Of particular interest to me about that assignment was the fact that students who couldn't write an essay to save their lives were suddenly in command of sentence structure and thesis development when writing a letter. Their problems with writing were obviously attitudinal, not cognitive. But that's another story.

It's worth noting that those of us who were involved in developing the digital citizenship field discovered that the term "digital citizenship" turned out to be somewhat problematic. An anecdote will help explain why. One time, during the Q&A portion of a digital citizenship presentation I was making to members of the general public, a gentleman raised his hand and asked, "So, when you are talking about being a digital citizen, do you mean versus being an American?" Therein lies the problem. The word citizenship can have a number of political connotations that the term "digital citizenship" does not share. Worse, any association with politics was only going to hinder our quest to help students develop the skills and perspectives they needed to use technology and the Internet in ways that were responsible, safe and inspired.

Mike Ribble, author of *Digital Citizenship in Schools,* and I led a number of discussions about revising the term digital citizenship with educators, during which we considered alternatives, like digital health and digital life skills. None of them resonated. Dropping the word "digital" simply didn't work for reasons I will address later on. Digital citizenship stuck.

I have recently heard another term used by technology integration specialist Jenn Scheffer: "digital maturity." To me, this captures the goal of digital citizenship succinctly, with breadth and depth, and without political overtones. I like it, and I hope it finds wide use.

As our team developed the early master's degree in educational technology, the question that drove us during times of unprecedented change was, "What does it mean to be an educated person?" We knew that as technology changed, the answer to that question would change. We also knew that it was our responsibility to help students develop more than just technology integration strategies. They also needed to cultivate big picture perspectives in order to manage the unprecedented change that was coming their way. We wanted them to be passionate about the new kinds of learning that technology was making possible in the classroom. However, we also wanted them to be reflective about their passions. Passionate, reflective people are the kinds of neighbors we want in real life and in virtual reality.

The foundational idea behind balancing passion and reflection was the need to understand that every step forward in terms of technological power, opportunity, convenience and comfort exacted some kind of price. An educated person would want to know what that price was. Even better, she would want to be able to anticipate that price ahead of time. I wanted my students to be able to proact, not just react. I wanted them to be historians, nowists and planners.

The challenge with trying to be proactive is that the upsides of technology are very immediate, enticing and easy to see, while the downsides are usually quite discreet and often only unfold imperceptibly over time. We often aren't looking for technology's consequences because typically they are neither foreseen nor intended. We embrace automobiles because they get us places. Much later on we notice the environmental consequences and resource depletion they cause. As we try to understand technological impact, we live life much as McLuhan described by driving forward while looking in the rear view mirror. We gaze into the past to see where we have just been, when it is too late to plot a new course. Or as the philosopher Kierkegaard said, "Life can only be understood backwards; but it must be lived forwards."

As I said in an earlier presentation, a simple question we can always ask in order to understand technological impact is, how does a technology connect us and disconnect us? Or, more proactively, how will it connect and disconnect us? We must always make the assumption that there are no connections without disconnections. Eyeglasses, as wonderful as they are, disconnect us from the people upon whom we used to depend in order to be able to move around in our communities. Facebook connects me to cousins who live across the country and whom I never expected to hear from with any kind of regularity. Facebook also connects me to friends who live just down the street whom I seldom encounter in my neighborhood. Yet, Facebook also disconnects me from communicating with the people sitting right next to me in RL whether they are friends at a party or strangers at the coffee shop. There are no connections without disconnections, but we often only see the disconnections after we have field-tested new technology by adopting it. At that point, it is often too late to change either the technology or how we have infused it into our lives, if that's what we want to do.

The microwave oven is a great example of unintended consequences and delayed disconnections. My guess is that just about everybody listening right now has a microwave oven. If you don't, then you are quite an anomaly. The connections made by the microwave oven are very apparent. It connects us to time and individual flexibility we wouldn't have if we prepared meals in traditional fashion. However, it also disconnects us from the need to congregate for family dinner for logistical reasons. By using the microwave each of us can make dinner quickly, easily and individually. As a result, Junior can go to soccer practice and stay as long as he needs to, while Sis can go to advanced physics lab after school and stay as long as she needs to. And Mom and Dad can stay at work as long as they need to in order to meet those deadlines that just won't let them rest. This lifestyle is facilitated by technology that allows everyone to come home whenever they want and make dinner by themselves whenever they want–quickly, easily and individually.

Let me tell you how the impacts of the microwave oven can permeate real life. A few years ago my wife and I were shopping for a house after the real estate crash. The market was flooded with more choices than we could consider. As we walked through dozens of houses I began to recognize a pattern. The older homes had dining rooms, while the newer homes didn't. Instead, the newer homes had feeding troughs attached to the kitchen in the form of quick-eating areas and dinettes. The dining room had been replaced by a family room, the focus of which was a large screen TV. The dining room, which had served as a family gathering place for dinner and conversations during my youth, had been replaced by a room that demanded quiet because everyone was watching television. I can't draw a straight line from the microwave to the disappearance of the dining room, but I can certainly point in that direction.

But I shouldn't pick on the microwave. The refrigerator and the dishwasher also help us lead life quickly, easily and individually. It's an appliance conspiracy.

It behooves us to understand that, as McLuhan noted, technology amplifies. It puts human behavior through a megaphone and magnifies whatever is there, for better or for worse. We want our children, students and fellow citizens to understand that the Internet and modern technology provide the loudest amplifiers that humanity has ever created. Technology's magnifying properties make it imperative that our students become digital citizens who are capable of seeing the big picture and understanding how they contribute to creating that big picture. Yes, we want them to develop practical skills like how to be safe and responsible online, and to practice "netiquette" (online etiquette) and empathy in virtual worlds. However, those aspirations will fall into place more readily if we help them cultivate a larger perspective about the digital lifestyles they lead. That's where digital citizenship needs to start.

With that context and historical background in mind, on with the show.

Parents' Night–Advice for Talking to Digital Teens

If you don't mind, I'd like to cast you in the role of parents right now. My guess is that many of you are parents, or even if your kids are grown and gone, you are still their parents and are now maybe even grandparents. Or perhaps your kids have moved back in with you while they figure out what's next in their lives, and you are in re-parenting mode. If so, you're not alone. All of you should start a support group. I am sure those of you who aren't parents are well aware of what comes with the territory of being a parent. Regardless of our parental status, we all know some children. They're everywhere. You help educate them through your tax dollars. Our children are everyone's future.

When I talk to parents I find that if I give them the opportunity to speak freely about how they really feel about living in the digital age, they will tell me they are not only excited about its possibilities, but also afraid about their kids being online. Their apprehension stems largely from the fact that our children seem to operate in a very underground world when they are immersed in social media. We don't really know where they are. They can make multiple copies of themselves, rename themselves, assume different persona and go places we don't even know exist. You might actually be talking to one of your kids online and not even know it. Now that's a scary thought. Needless to say, this is all very new.

Allow me to provide a sense of just how different the online world can be. When I was growing up, my parents magically always knew where I was. My dad was particularly concerned about my whereabouts because he did not want me hanging out with a kid named Arnold, who was just one of those bad kids that made parents very nervous. He was the kind of kid who would put sand in his math teacher's gas tank because he thought the test he gave was too hard. My dad knew if I was ever going to try smoking cigarettes, it was going to be because Arnold peer pressured me into doing so. Understandably, my dad didn't want me socializing with him.

My dad was normally a really sweet guy. However, when it came to Arnold he became quite serious. Now and again at dinner he would affix his steely gaze on me and in his gravelly, no-nonsense voice would ask me, "So, have you been hanging out with Arnold today?" My father was a schoolteacher and understood the adolescent mind. Lying was out of the question. I'd stammer through a few words and then he'd say, "Look, I know you were hanging out with Arnold. Somebody called me from the Boys Club and said they saw you and Arnold walking down the street in front of the bowling alley." I remember thinking, "My god, he has spies everywhere." Using technology as simple as rotary dial telephones, our parents built networks that could track us very effectively. And track us they did.

I'm afraid the days of always knowing where our children are may be over. Once any of us enters the world of the Internet, it is easy to hide or get lost. What do we do about that? I'm going to pass on seven observations that I hope you will find helpful.

The first observation is that the most effective strategy for being a part of your kids' digital lives is to have such a great relationship with them that they want to talk to you about what they do. I know that sounds like such an obvious thing to say. But the reality is that if you want to know how your children spend their time in the immersive reality on the other end of their devices, then you are dependent upon them telling you about it. Yes, you can check their Internet history. Yes, you can get records of whom they call with their cell phones. You can even install keyboard readers on their devices that send you files of everything they type, and use the Cloud to track their whereabouts 24/7, physically and virtually. But using all of those monitoring tools introduces trust and respect issues that can be quite divisive. And practically speaking, even if you could get past those issues, would you have time to do any of this? And even if you did have time, you would never prevent students from doing an end-run around every monitoring system you use. These days our kids are incredibly clever when it comes to outsmarting whatever barriers we put between them and their social media. Creative problem solving, I think we might call it. They tend to game the system, particularly if they have no hand in framing the system. Remember this: We want them framing the system, not gaming the system. More about framing versus gaming later.

Our job is to keep our children thinking and talking. Thinking and talking. Aloud. To us. We continually need to put issues about living a digital lifestyle before them and engage them in conversations about those issues. Having your children tell you what they do online is the best source of information you're ever going to get about their virtual lives.

My second observation is that depersonalizing the conversation helps students feel comfortable talking to us. If you ask, "Do you have more than one identity on your social network," then you will receive a rather evasive answer. However, you will receive an entirely different answer if you ask, "Say, I'm just curious. Why do you think people want more than one identity on Facebook?" When you depersonalize the question, they don't feel threatened about having to reveal information about themselves. The result is that they actually do begin to reveal information about themselves.

Third, we need to help our students and children develop meta-perspectives about their digital lifestyles. That is, we want them to step back from the screen and think about what it means to engage online, and how online interaction differs from real life communication. We want them to think about how their digital lifestyles connect and disconnect them. Depersonalizing the conversation is the first step in helping them do so. We want them to cultivate a big picture perspective about blending real life (RL) and immersive reality (IR). We want to keep them thinking and talking. Thinking and talking. Reflecting on the big picture. We should always be drawing them back from the screen, asking them to see their lives in a larger context.

Fourth, we need to always ask for their perspective. We want to know how they view the world. We need to learn from each other. It's all about the conversation. Most importantly, we need to make sure that when we do ask for their perspective that we honor their expertise. I'm not saying we have to agree with what they tell us. But we do need to thank them for their insight. This is how we keep the conversation going. The reality is that we are probably learning a great deal from them and genuinely will want to thank them for their perspective.

Fifth, we need to bring them to the policy table. If I could change one aspect about how we approach digital citizenship in school–that is, if I could just wave my hand and change something really big–it would be this: Adults would stop making all the Internet rules for students. Of course, we should be involved. But when we make all the rules, we rob our students of the opportunities they need and deserve to develop meta-perspectives, to see the bigger picture and to apply their understanding of the bigger picture to themselves and the digital lifestyles that they live. If we don't ask them to help frame the system, they tend to game the system. That is, when we make the rules, it's "game on" for them in terms of figuring out how to circumvent those rules. But, when the rules are their rules, their approach shifts. They tend to become much more adult and conservative in their perspective.

To help students frame the system, I engage them in an activity called *You're in Charge,* in which I put students at the policy table and ask them to develop policies related to digital lifestyle issues. I have done this with many age groups, from middle school to graduate students. I present them with an issue or a technology and ask, "What would you do about this? What should the rules be?" The issue could be how to handle a cyberbullying incident, or whether we should allow iGlasses and augmented reality (AR) in school, or whether it is okay for students to use neurologically enhancing headware that can actually help us "think better." Remember your teacher telling you to "put on your thinking cap?" Apparently version 1.0 of this technology has been developed. I ask students, "Should we allow this in school? Under what conditions?" They will face issues like these one day, if not as students, certainly as adults and parents.

When I engage them in these kinds of activities, an amazing thing happens: They go from gaming the system to framing the system. I watch them step into a broader, more responsible part of their minds.

Involving them in rule making has very practical value. Because they own the rules, they are much more likely to respect them. Also, it helps them develop the real skills they will need to navigate the rapidly evolving ethical grey areas created by emerging technologies. The reality is that you can't go anywhere virtually, or do anything digitally or technologically, without encountering tremendous ethical implications. We all need to be prepared to deal with this reality.

It might seem like this situation has nothing but downside. Another way to view it is to see the tremendous opportunity that it presents. Never before have students had so many opportunities to develop their ethical selves, and to understand their role in shaping the world as it could become. In order to turn this from theory into reality we need to seize the initiative. If we don't, then the digital citizenship issues we face will become nothing but a huge festering thorn in our side. Let's use the opening that emerging technology presents us to develop our moral perspectives. Let's ask students to help frame the system. We'll look at specific *You're in Charge* activities a little later.

Sixth, we need to triangulate. That is, we want home, students and school to converge on our digital citizenship efforts. Leaving digital citizenship to schools alone won't work.

I don't find much disagreement with this perspective. Most school community members I speak with tell me that digital citizenship is too vast to be just a school concern. In his book, *Digital Citizenship in the Schools,* Mike Ribble outlines "the nine elements of digital citizenship." He does an excellent job of capturing how much territory digital citizenship covers and how challenging it can be to create an in-depth program that addresses all of its components. The territory is so extensive that schools could devote their entire curricula to helping students become ideal digital citizens. Come to think of it, that's not a bad idea. Our efforts would still need parental and community participation to be truly effective. Regardless of how expertly a school approaches digital citizenship, the world that digital citizenship addresses travels with students beyond school, wherever they go, and is a part of nearly every activity in their lives. This fact alone makes it too pervasive to be just a school concern.

The point is that networks cross all boundaries. The BYOD "bring your own device" movement ensures that students take their second lives with them wherever their first lives go, through their laptops, smart pads, phones and whatever connected, wearable technology finds its way into their lives in the future. Whether students are at home, at school or are out socializing, they access the same social media and online resources. It's one seamless virtual life to them. We need parents, students and schools on board with the same policies and perspectives. We need to support each other.

Seventh and lastly, we want students to be aware rather than afraid of their digital lifestyles. I understand the pull toward wanting kids to be afraid of the harmful elements of the Internet. Hearing one heartbreaking story about a child who was abducted because she trusted someone on the Internet is all that it takes to inspire justifiable fear. But when our students understand the cautions, rather than just heed them, they have a better chance of transferring their understanding to new situations, or at least recognizing warning signs so that they can seek help.

Also, we need to help them cultivate a special, multi-faceted kind of awareness that consists of three primary components: Our students need to be informed, savvy and empathetic.

They need to be informed because they need to know what is going on, of course. But they also need to be savvy in that they need to know what is *really* going on. The flat, disincarnate world of text, as well as the reincarnate world of avatars, demand that we all try twice as hard as we normally would in RL to discern what transpires in our online environments. Simple observations can ground us in this regard. We need to look at who else is in our online environment with us. We need to consider the kind of language they use and the things they talk about. We need to scrutinize the ads we are pitched, and ask ourselves why we are being presented particular surveys and bombarded with particular pop ups. These elements paint a picture of the online space we are in. They provide subtext and tell us the story behind the story. In 1991, I introduced the term "online anthropology" at an anthropological association conference to a room of blank stares. It wasn't my best career move. The reality is that we all need to be online anthropologists in order to understand the reality and ethos of our online communities if we want to be savvy online citizens.

The third kind of awareness that students need to cultivate is empathy, which Merriam Webster defines as, "the feeling that you understand and share another person's experiences and emotions." Empathy skills have always been important. It's hard enough to understand someone you are talking to face to face. (I appeal to all of you in the audience who are in relationships to support me in this.) When we add a layer of electronic distance, empathy becomes an art form.

To illustrate this point with a group of students, I use an activity in which I ask each of them to articulate the phrase, "What do you mean?" with a different nuance and meaning. I have involved as many as twenty students in this activity, each of whom found a different way to inflect this phrase with a unique interpretation. In the often flat or representational world of online communication, we need to try especially hard to understand how others nuance their communication and activities, and what they are really feeling and trying to tell us.

The potential for miscommunication online is more complicated than we might think. When I was actively researching online communities, one of my findings was that when we read an email, we are actually reading ourselves. The human condition dictates that we need to imbue everything that happens to us with meaning, or else we experience chaos. That means that when we read a sentence in an email like, "What do you mean?" we are unconsciously compelled to imbue it with a particular intonation, context and, ultimately, meaning. Where that meaning comes from is the stuff of deep psychology. What is important here is that we project our meaning into the communication and then we read what we have projected as though it represented objective truth. Obviously, the potential for misunderstanding in our online world is very great. In that world, practicing empathy becomes not only a nice thing to do but also a survival skill we all need to develop. Misunderstanding someone because of our own projections and internal inflections could be bad for business, as well as interpersonal relationships.

The larger theme behind my seven observations is simply that we want to give our students every opportunity to cultivate the best filter they're ever going to have, which is the one between their ears. The only way that they can do that is through practice. *You're in Charge* activities are great exercises to use in this regard.

Please don't wait for school to engage your kids in conversations about living a digital lifestyle. Do it at home. Open up the newspaper, Google News, or whatever you read or watch. Go to the technology section, pick out an interesting digital lifestyle topic and pitch it to your kids. I just checked my main news sources and found articles about libraries streaming books, as well as robots that could reproduce themselves without much help from us. With a bit of effort I am sure I could have found an article or two about cyberbullying or a privacy breach. Have a conversation with your kids about these kinds of issues. Ask them, what would you do if you were in charge? Would you get rid of the library and give everyone iPads? Should students be allowed to bring robot assistants to school? If you were in charge, how would you handle a cyberbullying incident? These kinds of issues constitute the advancing edge of digital citizenship. And the future is just getting started. When I ask students questions like these, I watch them engage in ways that are exciting and incredibly interesting. They develop perspectives that I don't think they have ever voiced to themselves or their peers, and which we all need to hear. We need to keep them thinking and talking. Thinking and talking. These conversations should be a staple of public narrative.

Some Media Psychology

Now, I'm going to draw on my work as a media psychologist.

Youth face a neurological limitation when it comes to developing ethical perspectives. The prevailing notions about brain development these days say that the frontal cortex, where our ethical reasoning resides, is not fully developed until sometime in our early 20s. It seems ludicrous to think that we have to wait until we are in our 20s to make an ethical decision. And yet, truth be told, we all know people who have problems making ethical decisions all their lives. Sometimes it's an embarrassing family member. Let's move on.

A particular manifestation of an underdeveloped ethical center is disinhibition. This term refers to not being fully aware of the fact that we are engaged in activities in public that would be better reserved for a private space. If you are uninhibited, then you are dancing on top of a table, you know people are watching, and you don't care. If you are disinhibited, then you are dancing on top of the table and you either forget you are in public or honestly don't believe that others can see you. We are very disinhibited online. We tend to lock on to the person with whom we are chatting or texting and forget that we are in an amphitheater, making our thoughts available not only to our friends and colleagues, but also to the strangers who might read them or simply stumble upon them, pass them around and add them to our digital footprints.

We obviously need ethical reasoning much earlier than our twenties. The experts that I speak with tell me that the most effective way to jumpstart the development of our ethical reasoning skills is through practice. Once again, we return to the issue of student involvement. Our students need to be able to practice ethical reasoning. This is the only way to improve their abilities as ethical thinkers. If we make all the rules for our students, and don't at least involve them in exploring and developing those rules, we take away their practice opportunities.

While we're at it, I want to clearly voice my support for teachers serving as ethical coaches. I know this is a controversial topic. Some parents simply don't want teachers dealing with ethical issues with their children beyond a very basic level. They claim it's their business, not the school's business.

However, their concerns do not serve our students well. Our students need us engaged in their moral development. Toward that end, teachers need to have the latitude to address ethical issues associated with being online and using new technologies as they emerge. If teachers need training to help them to become more effective ethical coaches, then let's provide them the training they need. But let's completely infuse them into the process of helping students make ethical choices.

Zooming Out–Character Education and the Ideal School Board

Okay, now let's zoom out.

Let's explore a topic in greater depth that I touched on in an earlier presentation: the concept of "the ideal school board." Suppose that an ideal school board emerged somewhere on the planet. I can dream, can't I? These school board members woke up one day and decided they didn't really get the digital lifestyle thing. Many of them didn't grow up with it and don't understand it. The younger board members adopted it unconsciously, the way my generation unconsciously adopted a world of machines, like refrigerators and automobiles. After all, as long-time technology innovator Alan Kay says, "Technology is anything that wasn't around when you were born." Our ideal school board wants to take the best approach possible in its efforts to create a digital citizenship program. Therefore they begin by admitting their knowledge deficiency and start looking for help.

After conducting extensive research, our enlightened school board members have come to a foundational conclusion: Programs that approach digital citizenship as a "list of don'ts" aren't very effective. Further, addressing digital citizenship one issue at a time, from cyberbullying to privacy to copyright infringement, is exhausting and disconnected. Make no mistake — discussing and developing strategies to deal with specific issues is certainly important. However, as the technology evolves, new issues will always emerge. In fact, the individual issues are really symptoms that are challenging us to think deeper and more broadly. An overall approach to the issues needs a foundation, a context, a big picture. Based on its research, our ideal school board decides that what it really needs to do is develop a character education program attuned to students living digital lifestyles.

Character education has been around for quite a while and is predicated on the belief that academics and character are equally important in the education of our youth. Typically, character education programs are built on publicly defined values, which are then infused throughout the school community, from activities to curriculum. Character education is also built on the belief that our students learn character from all of us as a matter of course, simply from how we interact with them. You know the old saying, "Our children don't listen to what we say, they learn from what we do." If we're going to teach character anyway, why not do so deliberately? The net result of developing a goal-oriented character education program is to create a framework that better enables a school community to address specific issues of behavior and perspective.

To appreciate the importance of this approach, a brief history of character education might be helpful.

From about Plato until Eisenhower–I never thought I would use those two names in the same sentence–society assumed character education would be taught at school. Teachers might use anything from Bible stories to morality tales to homespun common sense in order to drive home points of character. Somewhere during the 1960s this approach to character development yielded to a period often referred to as morals clarification during which each of us was expected to clarify our own values, whatever they might be.

The subtext here was that perhaps mainstream culture's sense of character and values didn't resonate with everyone. If you belonged to one of the disenfranchised social groups in the 1960s, or had any awareness of their situation, then this made great sense. Common ground doesn't always serve everyone equally. Defining one's moral principles can clarify grievances to the general public that are based on differences in ethical priorities and social perspectives.

The price we paid in pursuing this approach, is that we lost some of our common footing. We could no longer assume that traditional moral perspectives would be acceptable in a public institution. From the 1970s until now there have been attempts to regain the common ground through the development of character education efforts here and there. Special programs have emerged, but the range of those programs has been limited to the schools that adopted them.

Sometime during the 1990s, considerations of character gradually became defined, in part, by the ethics of living a digital lifestyle. This development crept up on us without our noticing. It began by requiring signed agreements from students and parents that promised that students would behave well online. Asking students to sign character agreements was new. After all, students weren't signing them to be able to play on the playground. Then, before we realized what hit us, we were massively interconnected, mobile and immersed in two lives at once, with all of the ethical implications these developments imply. Suddenly the issues started coming at us: sexting, cyberbullying, illegal downloading, secording–which is secretly recording someone or something–and on and on. We found ourselves instantly overwhelmed. And the future was just getting started.

Today that brings us to the need to develop character education programs that are deliberately tuned to our digital lives. If we are smart, and we have an eye on the future, we will begin our digital citizenship efforts by developing a character education foundation attuned to the digital age and then build our digital citizenship programs on top of that. This approach will allow us to look more broadly and deeply at issues related to the virtual domain and the world of technology, as well as the arena of interpersonal relationships that are mediated by electronic communication.

Two Ethical Camps. Before I go any further, allow me to digress about an important point: Do we need new ethics just for a digital lifestyle, or can we simply use the moral and behavioral frameworks that our parents and grandparents taught us? Great question. It's not easy to answer.

I find there are two camps of thought regarding this question. Camp one says, "Just because we're talking about the digital domain, we don't need special kinds of considerations for ethics or character education. Doing right is doing right. Whatever works for real life will work for our new virtual and immersive domains as well." In contrast camp two says, "Let's be realistic. Immersive reality, as well as living in two places at once, has created a new world that invents new behaviors with complex moral implications we have not dealt with before. We are mashups of ourselves, managing our relationships in multiple dimensions. Of course we need some new approaches to ethics."

My heart is with camp one. I would like to be able to apply the ethics that my parents taught me to virtual reality and not need anything more. However, I am a realist. The fact is that life in the digital domain is different enough to warrant a number of special ethical considerations. Therefore, my head is with camp two.

Let me give you an example of the degree to which camps one and two differ. Consider the nature of theft. Back in the day, if I stole your car then I had your car and you didn't. Today if I download one of your photos, you probably don't even know that I have it because you still have your copy. As a matter of fact, you have an unlimited supply of your photo, as does everyone else with an Internet connection. As a matter of fact, if I use an image editing program to modify your photo to such a degree that it doesn't compete with your original, then, according to a legal consideration known as transformation, it's quite possible that I own it. At least that's where the law stands today. I can't do any of this with your stolen car.

Another important difference between conventional theft and downloading a photo is that whenever people steal cars they have a gut level feeling of some sort to go along with it. It might be guilt. It might be elation because they feel that their victim had it coming. But it is an emotion and it is probably an intense emotion. I don't think that happens when most of us download a photo. These days we tend to just grab and forward whatever interests us and not even think about it. We don't feel guilty because we don't even recognize that we're doing it. It has become normal behavior. How we think about this kind of behavior resembles how we think about jaywalking. We might know it's illegal, but we looked both ways, saw no one coming, and made what we consider to be a responsible decision given the circumstances. Similarly, the best of us reference the web sources we use and move on.

We have evolved into a culture of sharing and participation. This evolution is a natural extension of living a networked lifestyle. Our activities are framed by the expectation that we are going to use each other's material, mash it up and toss it around the Internet. If we don't like this arrangement, then what's our problem? Are we anti-social?

It's as though the default has flipped 180 degrees. It used to be, "You don't use my stuff and I won't use yours, unless we give each other expressed permission to do so." That was back in the day when it was very difficult to copy, alter and forward each other's materials. The new landscape seems to be, "We will use each other's stuff without asking unless we have expressly made clear that our work is proprietary." I call this area of inquiry UOPS (pronounced YOU-ops). It stands for "using other people's stuff." The term UOPS more accurately captures what we are dealing with here than the term "theft."

Let's not miss this opportunity to talk about citing our sources. I require my master's and PhD students to cite whatever sources they use in their own work. Citing sources is fairly easy to do within the very small bubble of academia, in which scholars tend to read and cite journal articles written by other scholars. Professional academic organizations like APA and MLA have developed structured approaches to referencing materials that have been used for many years.

But let's consider an average mashup I could create. I might start by taking a picture, which I manipulate with an image editor by splicing in a different background comprised of someone else's photo, which I then stretch in order to make it go "full screen," which I then modify in order to give it a "film noir" look. Then I put some music behind it using GarageBand or another audio editing program. The music is comprised of some pre-packaged loops that I altered, to which I have added some original guitar. I might add someone else's music I have sampled, as well as music I have downloaded from a free music site. In both cases I have edited and added original instrumentation to them. Is this original music? I call it "ouriginal." I might then include the entire composition in a movie, where I add more effects, before making it part of a PowerPoint presentation. Then I share it within yet another presentation format, like Google+ or SlideShare. Given that the medium is the message, this alters the meaning of the work at least somewhat. Cite that, I dare you. It doesn't matter whether or not everything I used to create my mashup is in the public domain. I always want to give credit to artists, regardless of whether they demand it or not.

We can use APA format, or at least we can try. However, if the point of citing our work is to inform the audience about the origin and nature of the compositional elements we use, as well as to respect the authorship of all those involved, then using APA format won't help us much. Trying to use a conventional citation approach to reference the components of a mashup leaves me feeling like I am trying to jam a square peg into a round hole. We need a new system. I think one of the most interesting and helpful tasks we could ask our students to undertake is to develop citation scheme 2.0. For now, if my students can't find a way to use existing citation systems to cite mashups and other digital projects, then they are free to develop their own. They often come up with approaches that are clearer than anything in use today.

UOPS and the world of fuzzy theft leave us in a very different world than the one we were used to back in the day, when theft was easily recognized and victims were clearly identifiable. Now we are not sure who's a thief, who's an artist and who is simply living a mashed up life that most consider normal. If we are going to help students understand their world, then we at least need to consider the kinds of ethical concerns that new situations like these present. We can't let our emotional attachment to the past keep us from providing the training and perspective they need to navigate the issues of living a digital lifestyle. That's why my head is solidly in camp two. Just to be clear, this is not to say that the ethics of the past aren't in play today. They are more important than ever. However, they need to be adapted and repurposed if they are to provide the same level and quality of guidance today and in the future as they have in the past.

End of the discussion about the two camps. Back to the enlightened school board.

Missions and Standards. I want you to imagine that our ideal school board is hard at work developing a mission statement. Using character education as a basis, its first attempt reads as follows: "Students will study and evaluate the personal, social and environmental implications and impacts of every technology and media application they use in school."

I like it. But of course I would; I wrote it. Although it sounds obvious and harmless, good luck finding a school district that has a mission like this one. Here's another mission statement bullet point: "Students will use technology and the Internet effectively, creatively and wisely. They will learn not only how to use them but also when and why, with a sense of safety, community, fairness and responsibility."

Again, it sounds entirely reasonable, but is very difficult to find. Here's another one. It's my favorite: "Students will learn to use technology and the Internet safely and responsibly while maintaining a sense of inspiration and opportunity about the value of both in their lives."

I particularly like this one because it recognizes the fact that living a digital lifestyle can be both problematic and valuable. Digital citizenship efforts can easily degenerate into a list of "don't do" activities. This mission statement acknowledges that the positive, empowering influences of technology need to be part of the vision.

Let's say that adopting a new mission isn't going to happen anytime soon in your particular situation for a number of strategic, bureaucratic or political reasons. What are your options? I suggest you begin exploring whether you can blend elements of the kinds of mission statements I have presented with your existing school values and missions. Many school districts have adopted character values in some form. Some districts give them a good deal of play. In other districts they're all but forgotten. However, generally they exist, you just need to find them. You might discover that all you have to do is tweak the character values that your school already recognizes to reflect digital lifestyle considerations. Following that adjustment, a character education program could be developed.

Let's try modifying an existing mission statement. If you go to missionstatements.com–yes, such a site exists–you can find mission statements collected from a number of schools. They make for fascinating reading. Here is one that was created by a middle school: "At our school our mission is to provide a safe environment, which promotes respect and motivates students to learn and to act responsibly. We believe education is the shared responsibility of the student's home, school and community." It sounds like a mission statement. It is vision driven and idealistic, as mission statements should be. I have yet to see a mission statement that says, "Mediocre is okay with us. We want students to be somewhat safe and a bit responsible. If half the students get passing grades, then we're happy."

For its purposes, our ideal school board might change this mission just slightly to read: "At our school our mission is to provide a safe environment, which promotes respect and motivates students to learn and to act responsibly *within their local and online communities.* We believe education is the shared responsibility of the student's home, school and community."

Not everyone is comfortable with something like this. It's just too...digital. And yet, we live in two places and we need to recognize that fact.

If I am making a presentation about character education and digital citizenship to school community members, I will sometimes use the school's value statement that I find posted on its public website as the basis for discussion. We evaluate what the district already has accomplished and what else it might need to do. Usually the conversation is spirited and sometimes uncomfortable. But it is always important and necessary.

Just so you know that character education missions do exist, I had the pleasure of working with Saint Michael's School in Santo Domingo in the Dominican Republic. One of the reasons they contacted me was because they had already embraced character education. They had read my book, *Digital Community, Digital Citizen,* about applying character education to digital lifestyles, and thought I would be a good fit to help them transition their values to the digital domain. Their mission reads, "We are committed to being a unique educational institution that combines academic excellence with a sound character education program to help students become principled lifelong learners and positive leaders who make a difference in the world." Well done. It provides a solid basis for migrating to the world of digital lifestyles. Unfortunately, it is one of the few references to a character education program in a mission statement that I've seen.

Let's return to our enlightened school board. Let's say it has developed its mission statement and now wants to get really practical. What steps could it take next? When I wrote *Digital Community, Digital Citizen,* I identified Character Education Partnership's (CEP) eleven principles of effective character education as the best source of character education standards. With CEP's permission, I adapted some of their principles to issues associated with students living digital lifestyles. Let's see what that looks like. Here is CEP's first principle:

1. Promotes core ethical values and supportive performance values as the foundation of good character.

This might become:

1. Promotes core ethical values and supportive performance values as the foundation of good character *in all communities, local, global and digital.*

Again, I think this might make people uncomfortable. My proposed modification merely acknowledges that our students live in two places at once, and suggests that there are new issues of character to consider because of it. But it's still a little unsettling to hear it out loud.

Let's look at another of the eleven principles of the Character Education Partnership. Principle number four reads:

4. Creates a caring school community.

This might become:

4. Creates a caring school community, *including social media communities that are a part of school activities.*

The only reason that I suggest limiting this principle to just school activities is because schools can't effectively be held accountable for what happens beyond school. At present, online activities that overlap school and the world outside school fall within a very murky legal area. Our second, immersive life follows us everywhere and yet our traditional approach to school behavior is largely geographically based. Here's how confusing the situation can become. Students can access their online lives via their laptops at school. In this case they are physically at school using the school's equipment and network to be virtually someplace else. But they can also access their online lives using their own cell phone network rather than the school's network. In that case, they are in the school's physical space using their own equipment and network to access their virtual space, which may or may not be related to school activities.

We have not caught up with the fact that we live in two places wherever we go and that the second place is basically the same regardless of where we are physically located. But even enlightened school boards don't want to become responsible for all student behaviors wherever they occur. So for now, school boards are concerned primarily with what happens while students are physically at school.

Let's consider another approach to adapting CEP's work to our needs. Perhaps we leave the principles intact and simply add a twelfth principle. Maybe the new principle reads something like, "All the preceding principles apply to both onsite and online environments and behaviors."

Or maybe we just leave the eleven principles intact and expand the evaluation criteria that are used to determine whether we are meeting the standards. CEP's principles of effective character education provide evaluation criteria that operationalize each principle in real terms. That is, CEP identifies particular conditions and behaviors to look for to determine the degree to which a school is CEP compliant. For example, let's consider principle number four, "creates a caring school community." Perhaps our school board adds the following to the existing list of assessment criteria:

1. Uses netiquette
2. Practices empathy in virtual communications
3. Helps others in virtual settings
4. Shares technical expertise

If we just expanded the evaluation criteria, we might be able to leave the rather timeless eleven principles alone. This approach might also help our students blend their two lives into one integrated approach to living.

Branding Your Digital Citizenship Program

What else might our ideal school board do? I strongly recommend that schools and organizations develop a brand for their digital citizenship efforts. That is, they need to describe what is truly important to them about digital citizenship in one sentence.

Why a brand? One of my favorite speakers is Guy Kawasaki. In one of his presentations he claimed that he could walk into most organizations and ask most anyone he met to tell him the organization's mission statement, and very few could do so. He said the reason for this is that mission statements are too long. According to him, what every organization needs is a mantra that speaks to what is truly important to that organization and is short enough for anyone to memorize.

Developing a brand can be a very simple first step in

building an effective digital citizenship program. The area that digital citizenship covers is so vast that it's very difficult for any school district to address all aspects of it, regardless of how enlightened its school board might be. However, a school district could develop a brand as a starting point to help all school community members navigate large parts of it. Let's try saying what is important to us in a sentence.

To be very clear, that one sentence is what we would use to facilitate conversations between students and teachers, students and students, teachers and parents, each other, and among any members of a school community. Make your brand easy to remember so it can begin the conversations that you need to have.

I love to lead digital citizenship brand development discussions among stakeholders. They are always spirited and enlightening. Frequently, some in the brand development group will suggest something like, "Use the internet safely, respectfully and responsibly." Typically, others will respond with comments like, "That sounds like we're preaching. How about we add, 'with a sense of inspiration, creativity and purpose?'" Then there are those who want to make sure that we mention using the Internet honestly and fairly. Others want to add *protectively.* This was a new word for me. It describes the very real, practical desire to have students protect themselves and each other on the Internet. It is up to students to say to their friends, "What you're doing right now isn't safe." They need to feel comfortable doing this. It is their brand, too.

There are those pragmatists who say let our brand simply be, "Don't post anything on the Internet you don't consider publishable." The concern about being publicly and virtually visible goes to the heart and soul of the digital footprint or digital tattoo, which we're going to address a little later. As one person framed this issue, "Don't put anything on the Internet you wouldn't want your grandmother to read." I suppose whether or not this works depends on your grandmother. One of my grandmothers wouldn't dare show her ankles in public. It just wasn't done. But another bragged that when she was twelve years old she made good money using her little red wagon to transport illegal whiskey during prohibition. Perhaps we need a grandmother rubric. Let's move on.

Others feel the need to develop an acronym for their brand. One group wanted to adapt the THINK acronym that's in wide use: true, helpful, inspiring, necessary, kind. Another suggested using the acronym SCIE (pronounced "sky"): Safe, Civil, Informed, Engaged. And so on. Obviously, there are many approaches to developing a brand for your organization.

The point here is that digital citizenship is vast. That's why a simple brand can be a great place to start the conversation. It can provide a solid foundation, while promising to be flexible enough to adapt to new challenges as technology evolves.

Quite often I assume the role of narrative researcher when I work with brand development teams. Following a short presentation by me about digital citizenship issues and the basics of branding, it's up to participants to talk about their goals and their process. I take notes. If the timing works out, I will conduct a narrative analysis of their conversation over lunch or during a break. Narrative analysis is one of my areas of specialization as an instructor in Fielding Graduate University's Media Psychology PhD program. My job is to deconstruct the conversation, then break it down into its elements and themes. Basically, my job is to tell clients what they're actually saying, and to synthesize it into two or three main points.

The results of one branding team that I worked with is particularly helpful to our discussion here. In their case I heard school community members make two primary points, which ended up becoming what they called their guiding principles. First, it was important that every teacher be considered a digital citizenship teacher. That is, the committee members didn't want just certain teachers to be responsible for teaching digital citizenship. Everybody needed to share that responsibility and opportunity. Although they looked forward to working with specialists who could help with issues of copyright, cyberbullying and so on, they didn't want to leave the education, implementation and enforcement of digital citizenship just to specialists.

The second guiding principle was that a digital citizenship program required both specific units of instruction and general infusion throughout the curriculum. A key concept here is that it would be up to teachers to infuse digital citizenship into their curricula, again, returning to the idea that every teacher is a digital citizenship teacher. Teachers could achieve this by asking a number of questions at the end of a unit of instruction like: How does this technology connect us and disconnect us? Were there any issues of privacy or security associated with what we did today that we should address? How did the technology that we were using disrupt social, environmental or community relationships? If one digital citizenship area is particularly relevant, then focus there.

Then branding team members fleshed out their two guiding principles with some detail. Members added the following to the first point: "The discussion of digital citizenship provides a rich learning opportunity. Teachers should be looking for the digital citizenship aspect of whatever they're doing." Number two was clarified with the following: "Digital citizenship requires units of instruction and infusion. We should use a variety of approaches and curriculum. Tech learning coordinators can design curriculum parameters of digital citizenship to help teachers infuse digital citizenship within their curriculum." What we see here are roles not just for teachers but also for curriculum developers. A digital citizenship program is a team effort.

Then I presented these results to another school, with the

first school's permission of course. Participants said, "We really like what they have done, but want to add one more guiding principle. Every parent is a digital citizenship teacher." It made perfect sense to me, and echoed my earlier point about triangulation.

Once you have developed your guiding principles, then you can become very practical about your training and professional development needs including: how to use guest presenters, what kind of home-to-school connections you want to develop, whether to provide training for parents and so on.

Before I leave this area, I will pass on an observation that has seemed to be consistent over the years: What teachers really want is curriculum. I find that most teachers care about digital citizenship, but they don't know where to begin.

More importantly, they want mini-curriculum tailored to an already busy school day. Current trends in alternative forms of evaluation, like micro credentials and badges, may encourage the development of these kinds of materials. Given the time demands of testing and Common Core mandates, most schools are not going to have the flexibility in their schedules to be able to implement a separate digital citizenship curriculum of any magnitude. However, they might be able to consider using mini lessons that could be introduced during literally any topic, in any course. I mentioned this above in terms of teachers taking a moment to ask students about digital citizenship issues that were involved in the day's material. Teachers can tailor this approach to whatever is going on at their school or in their classrooms. If piracy is a big issue, then talk about piracy. If students are downloading web materials for a course presentation, then focus on the issues associated with doing so. The point is that I don't see education opening up large swaths of time for digital citizenship coursework any time soon. That means that educators will need to infuse it into their daily work. They can do that to some extent by asking students to reflect on digital citizenship considerations within the context of classroom activities. To keep the public in the loop, I recommend creating a public blog that discusses these issues. This kind of resource would expand the discussion beyond school, and involve everyone in the digital citizenship conversation.

Student Activities

Our enlightened, ideal school board members have come a long way and learned a great deal. Now they shift their focus to student activities. This is where the rubber meets the information highway. Let me share some activities with you that I would most certainly share with them. Most of the activities I am going to describe have been used with students at all levels, from middle school to PhD. I use them with students, administrators, community members…literally anyone.

I like to begin digital citizenship exercises with an activity about digital footprints, which some call digital tattoos because of the permanence of the residue they leave behind. Others call them digital scrapbooks, a term that describes how we present ourselves online very well. We build our scrapbooks across social media in transmedia fashion. We collect as we go, often in an unorganized, unconscious and uncoordinated fashion. However, over time our activities coalesce into a recognizable web presence, looking very much like a distributed scrapbook.

We have all heard the horror stories about people losing their jobs and their friends because of a Tweet gone wrong or an inappropriate party photo going viral. In fact, we owe it to ourselves to be careful with our online persona. Human resource personnel do Google us and do search Facebook and social media for us, looking for warning signs. The reality is that if you are competing with somebody for a job and the two of you are functionally equivalent–that is, you both have equivalent degrees, great work records and five years of experience–but you have posted some compromising pictures or used language that doesn't seem professional on social media, then the job is going to go to your competitor. When employers have a choice, they are obligated to make the smarter choice. Given what may have been posted about you on social media, that employer's choice may not be you. When I'm working with students, I play compelling videos that explain the pitfalls of inappropriate web exposure very well. You can find many of them on YouTube with a simple search.

The threat of a negative digital footprint is only part of the story. My focus with students is to flip the situation around and ask them to approach their digital footprints from a deliberate and positive point of view. If we plan to make our true identities available online, rather than hide through aliases and screen names, then we have agreed to enter into a world in which we can no longer hide. In this situation we can either live in fear of how the world sees us or we can shine on the world stage. Rather than just thinking in terms of what we shouldn't post, let's think in terms of telling our story the way we want it told. We need to ask, "How is it we would like the rest of the world to see us?" Ultimately, this question amounts to, "Who do I want to be?" I get practical about this by having students design reflective e-portfolios that describe the best that they have to offer.

I appreciate that there are a number of issues about children maintaining a presence on the web. This is a thorny, grey area that pits a desire to have students present themselves positively on the web, with concerns for student anonymity and safety. Both approaches try to control the narrative, one through proactive involvement, the other through avoidance. Responses by schools and communities to this situation vary widely. Some cede to the reality that students are already embedded in the web and prefer to control and manage the situation by showing the world the good things their students do. Others allow no web presence at all for students, and often defer largely to parents and what they allow their children to do at home. Then there is everything in between. Every school is its own culture, and every culture sees this differently.

The reality is that students are on the web, often for academic and social reasons, certainly by middle school, sometimes earlier. By the time they are in high school we can assume they have some kind of recognizable presence on the Web. The question is, do they want to actively manage their online story or do they want others to tell their stories for them? I would suggest we all want to manage our online presence and not leave that to others. As I mentioned earlier, our online presence is our story to tell. We need to help our students and our children enter digital adulthood in this regard.

Even if we're skittish about students having an online presence, we can certainly require them to begin thinking in terms of presenting themselves to the world by collecting the kinds of work examples and personal and professional reflections they would include in an ePortfolio that may go live one day. Or, we could have them create online presences that exist on a server behind a firewall that are only accessible to people in the district, or parents, or employers, or by permission. A simple approach for older students is to create accounts on LinkedIn, a well-respected online social media platform without a lot of the chitchat or social foibles of Facebook. It distinguishes itself from other social media in this regard, and has become the online venue that employers, colleges and professionals turn to for networking purposes. These are just a few approaches. The bottom line is that if we can't hide anymore, then we have to manage the information about us that others find.

When I teach students about using the "positive portfolio" method, I often watch them struggle to identify the good things they do. They have a hard time thinking about their lives in terms of positive activities. I have to prod. I ask them questions like, "Do you volunteer anywhere? Do you create artwork? Do you create music? Are you on a sports team? Do you walk other people's dogs? Are you a part of a church or civic group? Do you recycle, hike, or take your health seriously?" And so on. In the process they often discover how awesome they are, as well as what they still need to accomplish.

The goal for them is to deliberately create their own story arc that begins today, or perhaps some time in the past, and stretches out to… they pick a time: When they graduate from high school? From college? In my presentation, *The Art of the Story,* I talk a great deal about stories, and how they are built on story arcs and the three points of the story core: challenge, transformation, resolution. For now what is important to understand is this: Transformation is key. Story heroes not only overcome challenges, but they also change in the process. So I ask students, "Who do you want to become, and what do you need to learn to get there?" It's a bit like asking, "What do you want to be when you grow up?" It's also a way of asking, "Who do you want to be when you grow up?" I ask them to set goals for themselves. Hopefully, they elect to make their goals part of their portfolios. Any effort they make to capture positive goals and accomplishments, and to reflect on changes they have made and need to make to move forward with their lives, is going to create a compelling online presence. If there happens to be some stuff online about them that is less than flattering–and bear in mind that it can even be stuff that someone else made up about them–then the good stuff will eventually drown out the bad stuff.

You're In Charge

I want to talk about the *You're in Charge* activities I

referenced earlier. They are some of the most powerful activities that I do. And the most fun. Recall that we need to make digital citizenship fun and interesting. It may not survive if we don't. I do *You're in Charge* activities with students of all ages, from youth to seniors.

The foundational concept behind this activity is the fact that technology is invisible to most people, particularly our digital youth, and we first need to see technology in order to take charge of it. Generally, we only really see technology when it breaks, appears out of context or we decide, for whatever reason, to focus on it. Allow me a brief aside about how one such "focusing" exercise changed my life.

I had the honor of listening to Marshall McLuhan hold forth during the 1970s at the University of Toronto. During one lecture he was a bit frustrated by the fact that we weren't getting the concept of "the medium versus the message." We just weren't understanding it because he was brilliant and we weren't. That's it in a nutshell.

What Dr. McLuhan was trying to explain was that our experiences consist largely of two components, content and medium, and that medium shapes content. The result is that technology shapes behavior. Or, as he is often credited with saying, "We shape our tools, and thereafter they shape us."

Consider the cell phone. Some content may be too detailed for the restrictions of a cell phone screen, while other content may be ideally and even exclusively suited for it. The nature of the screen, the interface and the connectivity determines what developers make available for each device. Because media shapes content, services like Facebook and Google create different interfaces for the different smart devices in our lives in order to avoid their limitations and play to their strengths. But you can't understand this unless you can separate the medium and message and see them as separate elements.

This day in class Dr. McLuhan said, "Everybody..." and I

challenge you to do this… "Everybody, pick up any piece of reading material you want. I don't care what it is–a magazine, a newspaper, a book, whatever you have. Turn it upside down. Now that you can't read it, you are beginning to notice it as a medium."

I was holding a textbook, which I promptly turned 180 degrees. Immediately, I began to experience it as an object rather than a book. It was a particular size. It was somewhat heavy. It contained lots of black squiggles on a white background. It was portable. Some of us had the same textbook, providing a community of sorts. As my class members and I were looking at the objects in our hands, we were effectively alone, using McLuhan's "private point of view." This was very different from the community storytelling experience we were enjoying at McLuhan's lecture. I suddenly understood McLuhan's concept of literacy as "trading an ear for an eye," as we moved from pre-literate to literate culture. Then he told us to turn whatever we were holding right side up and feel the shift in our brains. As I pivoted the book, the object in my hands melted away and became reading material once again. The shift in my brain was palpable, feeling like water sloshing from one side of my mind to the other. The book as a thing, as a medium, was gone. I was immediately sucked into the content–the message–and began reading. He said, "That is the medium versus the message. Understand?" And I understood. He taught me to see.

You're in Charge activities are really exercises in seeing and developing a meta-perspective about the medium of technology. To do this, students must focus on technology that is usually invisible to them. In McLuhan's language, they need to transform the technology in their lives from "ground"–the environment they don't notice–into "figure," something they can see and focus on. Students get a chance to do this when I put them in charge of technology and Internet policy for their schools. When they see technology, they tend to frame rather than game the system. The results are always inspiring.

My first activity typically focuses on "the math hat," my name for a particular kind of neurologically enhancing headware that apparently can massage your brain and improve your math aptitude. I love to pitch this technology to students first because it comes out of nowhere. It throws them completely off balance, and wakes them up. I explain what the math hat does, and then ask, "Should we allow math hats in school? Under what conditions? What should the policies be?"

I've collected notes over the years about how students have responded to the math hat. Frequently I hear a number of students say, "Are you kidding? Of course I want it if I'm going to get better math grades." But one student always steps forward to say something like, "I don't want it. It wouldn't be me. It would be fake. I want to know that I can do math on my own." Just one student making a comment like this encourages others to wade into the critical thinking arena to support her perspective. Then I might prod with something like, "But you use Excel and calculators. Is that fake?" Students often respond with comments like, "My calculator (smart phone) is with me wherever I go, but my math hat isn't." Or, "I would get used to it and when I didn't have it, I'd be math dumb."

They're also asked to develop policies about using the math hat. I hear ideas like, "It needs to be studied more to make sure that it's not harmful before we use it." Or, "As long as it is proven not to be harmful, then we can use it, but only when the teacher says so." Or, "We can use it only to study, not to take tests." I typically hear a comment like, "We can use it only if everybody has one." It's encouraging to hear students identify the very real possibility that the math hat could create classes of haves and have nots. Those who can't afford a math hat will be relegated to lower math achievement. One student cleverly called this situation "the hats vs. hat nots."

Then we move on to something that might be a little bit

more familiar, like Google Glass. Currently Google Glass is not in vogue, but I assure you it will return in some form. For now I will refer to this kind of device generically as iGlasses. I think it's fair to assume that sooner or later some form of iGlasses may be built into eyeglasses so they don't look so strange. They might be built into contact lenses, in which case we won't even know they are there. Whatever form they take, the question before our students is, "What rules do we need to guide our use of iGlasses at school?"

The responses are fascinating. Many students thought they should be able to use them to find out more information about what they were discussing in class, flickering their attention among the screen in their eyes, their colleagues and the teacher. Some also felt they shouldn't be able to use them during tests because they could look up answers, while others thought that doing so would demonstrate skills in digital literacy.

There were concerns about broadcasting, which iGlasses can do, particularly if those being broadcast didn't know about it. One student responded by saying, "But wouldn't it be great if we broadcast class to the Web because people might be home because they're sick or they're at a sporting event or something like that." Then someone would suggest something like, "If we go to a museum why shouldn't we broadcast from there so we can share it with the rest of the school?" Then someone might say, "Maybe it's not okay with the museum that you do that." This opens up a great avenue of discussion about intellectual property rights, respect in general, and, above all, where is school? Is school a set of buildings, the community or something that exists in the digital world? Or all of these? Are we always at school? Are we never at school? There are no definitive answers to these questions, but these are great questions to ask and great areas of inquiry to investigate. As long as students are asking questions like these, then I feel much better about the world that they are going to manage.

Another *You're in Charge* activity is related to the digital manipulation of photographs. There was a time when we were outraged when we discovered that magazines altered their photos. Now we prefer it. If we see an ugly photo we ask, "What happened to the Photoshop artist on this one?"

To set the stage for this activity I show students examples of digitally manipulated photos that I have collected over the years. Some photojournalists have done an excellent job documenting the "before and after" effects of Photoshopping, and provide a great portal into this world.

For dramatic effect I usually start with this photo of myself. That's me, long before I artificially died my hair white to give myself a professorial ambiance. The picture of me in photo A is the original. It was among the first photos to be posted

on a University of Alaska website. When I found out it had been made so public, I felt uncomfortable. Seeing my hand jammed into my pocket simply didn't look professional enough to be viewed by the rest of the world. So, I used Photoshop

version 2.0 to create photo B. Notice my hand now hangs neatly at my side. A technical note for you geeks out there: The version of Photoshop I used didn't support layers. I just heard a few people gasp. I think a few others fainted. Yes, it was ugly.

I preferred using the doctored photo to the original. How did I justify this? Simple. Had I known that this photo was going to be posted on the Web, I wouldn't have had my hand in my pocket when the picture was taken. So, the manipulated photo is actually more honest... isn't it?

The questions for students included, "Do I have a right to alter my own photo? Is there anything wrong here? Should the public be warned when altered photos appear in certain publications?" Initially, the students and I were interested in what happens only in school publications. But the conversation tended to go global very quickly. After all, most of the photos they were exposed to in the course of a school day came from media sources outside school. I often expanded this exercise by putting them in charge of the entire world of media. A scary thought, I understand. But their power was temporary.

One group of students with whom I was working decided the journalism trade needed a rating system. They felt that photographers and media organizations should be required to assign a number, from one to ten, that provided an indication of the degree to which a photo had been changed. For convenience, the number would appear in the lower right hand corner of the photo. Further, they wanted to require journalism organizations to provide readers with the opportunity to click on the photo and see the original, as well as read an explanation about how the photo had been altered. An ingenious idea.

Some of the most interesting conversations I have had with students have been about the qualifications they felt photo evaluators would need to have. After all, we will need evaluators to determine whether a photo is a three or a four. We can't just let anyone make these determinations, can we?

In one case I happened to be working with fourteen-year olds, a fact that will become important in a moment. A subgroup of the class that I had charged with considering the issue of evaluator qualifications made the following recommendation: Evaluators needed to be at least twenty-one. Well, that's as far as they got. The class erupted in disagreement. TWENTY-ONE?! Their peers all wanted to sit on the evaluation board and had been excluded because of their age. The subgroup quickly capitulated: fourteen was the new age to qualify for board membership. They also developed the following criteria: candidates must be fair; must be qualified to run for office (which would have raised the age, but it didn't seem important to point that out at the time); and–this is my favorite–they must be able to think correctly. That usually meant, "They should see the world the way I do."

Another subgroup worked on how to calibrate the rating system. What was a one? What was a five? A ten? Their initial efforts tried to calibrate by example. Perhaps eliminating the flash from somebody's eyes is a one, and putting the Queen's head on Elvis' body and making it look like he was flying would be a ten. Digitally manipulating my arm was maybe a five. And so on. They approached calibration more globally, too. They came up with interesting ideas, like rating a photo based on the number of pixels that had been changed, and evaluating a photo based on the degree to which the meaning of the photo had been altered. The conversations about what a photo means were priceless.

I remember thinking to myself that the rating system was a fabulous idea, but it would never happen. I thought that attempts to mandate altered-image labeling would be rejected as an abridgment of freedom of speech and artistic license. But then something like it did happen. A few years ago Israel passed a law known as the Photoshop Law that required advertisers to clearly identify ads that used digitally altered images of models. Rachel Adato, who helped champion the law, said "A revolution has begun…this law shatters the anorexic ideal serving as an example for the country's youth." Incidentally, the law also required that models working in print ads and runway shows had to meet a Body Mass Index threshold of 18.5. It turned out that my students not only had a great idea, but also a feasible idea.

This is exactly the kind of issue our students should be grappling with. Issues like this are everywhere and new ones emerge every time a new technology is born. But where do we find time to address these issues in our current approach to curriculum?

In the *You're In Charge* activities we also talk about cyberbullying, another area for which adults tend to create all the rules. I turn it over to the students and say, "What would you do if a cyberbullying incident was brought to your attention? You're the policy board. You're the enforcement board. What would you do?" As students, the appropriate answer is that they would report it to an adult. However, I ask them to just set that off to the side for a moment and imagine they actually were in charge. How would they respond?

They frequently prefer the direct confrontation approach. "Why are you doing this? Look what you've done. You need to apologize!" And so on. I watch students of all ages become very conservative. I'll never forget the day an eighth grader insisted that elementary students who were caught cyberbullying should go to jail; that would teach them. The reality is that when students frame the system, they have very little patience for those who game the system. They have little tolerance for those who abuse their media channels and tend to view destructive behavior as a type of vandalism of virtual space that is important to them. They move to a more adult viewpoint very quickly as they address these issues.

Also, they typically express concern about the actions of those who witnessed an incident. Were they bystanders who did nothing? Or were they outstanders, that is, people who actually responded to the incident? Interesting conversations ensue about what to do about bystanding. Most are punitive in nature. That is, students often recommend there be penalties for doing nothing.

Interestingly, the only time I have ever heard any kind of concern for the bullier was from a group of high school students. Their point was simply this: People are mean because their lives are unhealthy in some way. The bullier wasn't going to stop being mean just because his internet privileges were revoked; his issues would simply surface in another way. The students wanted to offer counseling to help him move past his anger. It was in his best interest as well as everyone else's.

We're just getting warmed up in terms of *You're in Charge* activities, but I'm running out of time, and there are two more activities that I want to describe: *Being a DeTECHtive,* and *Being Your Own Futurist.*

Being a DeTECHtive

The US Government funds the Food and Drug Administration, known widely as simply "the FDA." One of the FDA's primary duties is to determine the health and safety value of the food and drugs we consume before they are released to the public. Similarly, suppose there was a Science and Technology Administration (STA), whose job it was to determine the social, environmental and interpersonal consequences of new technologies before we could consider adopting them. What kinds of evaluations might the STA use?

Let me say that I hope the government never creates an STA, at least not one with punitive powers. It would kill innovation as we know it. However, I see great value in using an STA perspective as the basis for an educational activity to help us consider technology adoption in a more investigative, long-range way. Critical thinking, I believe it is called. The STA works as the basis for short mini-lessons, longer units of instruction, and everything in between. More importantly, teachers can use the STA as a touchstone in literally any area of study, allowing any teacher to become a digital citizenship teacher. As appropriate issues arise, teachers can ask students, "So, what would the STA say about this?" Those in the world of corporate and organizational responsibility also could use an STA perspective very effectively to sort through the myriad of ethical issues they confront on a regular basis.

Generally, I like to divide STA participants into three subgroups: the innovators, the STA investigators and a panel of judges. The innovators defend the innovation, the investigators question it, and the judges render a decision about whether society should have access to it. The reality is that I rarely have the time I would like, so I ask everyone involved in the activity to think as all three. Typically, the innovators present an established or contemporary technology as though it was new, or they present a technology they expect will exist at some point. The evaluation then uses seven criteria, which the students and I have discussed in preparation for the activity:

1. Physical characteristics—How is the technology made, what is it made of, how is it used, who fixes it when it breaks, etc.?
2. Enhancements/reductions—How does it amplify and diminish us?
3. Predecessors/next steps—What did it replace, and what does it imply?
4. Social contexts—What are the social expectations that produced our desire to have it?
5. Biases—Whom does it favor, and who is left out?
6. Benefits—What are the qualities of this technology that drive its creation and adoption?
7. Impacts—What are its connections and disconnections?

This is just a suggested list. Feel free to modify it as you see fit.

Evaluation is limited to three recommendations: accept, reject or accept with modifications. Some of my favorite moments as a teacher have been listening to students defend the pencil as innovators, while listening to evaluators' fears about a world of information overload that would ultimately be traced back to the distribution of such an inexpensive writing device. Another highlight was the time that a student passionately defended her right to take her robot to the prom, while evaluators insisted that the robot could not be part of a dance contest due to its physical advantages. There were also the energetic discussions about whether virtual reality simulations should be historically accurate, whether our genetic profiles should be public information, whether neuro-enhancement technology should be allowed in education and a number of other salient topics. I am just scratching the surface of this activity. However, I trust you get the idea.

Being Your Own Futurist

Lastly, I want to tell you about an activity that is always engaging called, *Being Your Own Futurist*. It explores digital citizenship from a proactive perspective by allowing participants to predict and design the future, based on an historical understanding of the impacts of technology. Developing this perspective allows participants to imbue the future with all the positive characteristics that digital citizenship supports. Briefly, here is how the activity works.

I present students two methods of predicting the future of technology: the linear approach, incrementally and disruptively, and the intersecting circles approach. The linear approach simply asks, "If older technology used to perform certain tasks one way, and today's technology performs those tasks in a new way, what innovational approaches to performing those tasks await us in the future?"

The suitcase is a great example of a technology that has evolved over the years and promises to keep developing long into the future. Young people in the audience will find this hard to believe, but at one point we carried our suitcases. That is, we actually picked them up off the ground, against gravity, and lugged them around using a handle. I will never forget the first time I saw someone rolling a suitcase down an airport hallway, a feat made possible by the fact that it was supported by two wheels. It was a religious experience. I had to have one. I remember thinking, "That should have been version 1.0 of the suitcase." A few years later I saw a demure, elderly lady, roll a suitcase about her size down a long stretch of airport hallway with very little effort. This was made possible by the fact that the suitcase had four spinner wheels. I had another religious epiphany, thinking, once again, "That should have been version 1.0 of the suitcase."

The questions that drive the *Being Your Own Futurist* activity are, "What's next? What is it that we aren't seeing now that will seem obvious in hindsight to us tomorrow?" We then deconstruct a technology's evolution in the order of its incremental changes. This helps us see the next steps that are likely to happen. Incremental change simply extends the current evolution of a technology rather than changing it radically. In predicting the future of luggage, it might mean the development of hovering suitcases, power-assisted suitcase wheels, or suitcases we control from a smart device.

Then we look at disruptive change, a term in current use to describe situations in which change produces something so different that it radically alters the business model and challenges the dominance of primary market players. In the example of the suitcase, perhaps Uber picks up our luggage and takes care of it for us, so we don't care how many wheels our suitcases have. Perhaps a special mail service overnights our bags for a reasonable price directly to our hotel, and that service simply becomes part of the hotel costs. Maybe the change is not so much in the suitcase but in what we carry in it. Maybe our packed items are specifically created to be lighter, making them easier to transport, a trend that is already underway. The goal of the activity is to imagine whatever it is we are not imagining right now. Let your imagination have fun.

The other approach I show participants for understanding innovation is the intersecting circles method. Technology is rarely entirely new, and almost always emerges as the result of combining existing technologies. It helps to think of this in terms of overlapping sets, like the kind we learned in modern math. Simply put, we ask, "What is produced when we overlap two technologies?" If we overlap an old fashioned suitcase with a wagon we get a suitcase on wheels. The car overlaps a perfume bottle, which became a carburetor, with Newcomen's steam engine, which became a motor, with Faraday's generator, which became an alternator, and so on. More recently, if we overlap a car with GPS and motion recognition we have automated cars, that are self-driving and that can be controlled using body movement. This technology is under rapid development.

Let's consider combining the Internet with motion technology, like the Wii or Kinect, and using one of the popular bowling programs they provide. The result makes it possible to play in a bowling league halfway around the world, or to take bowling lessons from experts from another country, or maybe even to bowl with our kids when we are away on business. Bear in mind that motion-driven technologies like

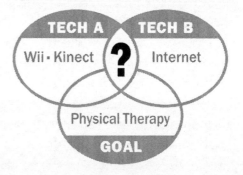

TECHNOLOGY INNOVATION GAME

these do much more than allow us to bowl. We can expand our activities to include dancing, playing golf, playing in a musical band, you name it.

Then we add a third circle to the intersecting circles approach in the form of a goal. Let's stick to connecting the Internet with a Kinect, and then add the goal of physical therapy. Perhaps doing so enables an expert in another country to read our movements for the purpose of therapeutic analysis. If we are lucky, maybe the expert is also a golf pro, and also provides free golf lessons. Again, let your imagination have fun. Behind most technologies you will find an intersection of existing technologies, driven by a goal. This fact allows us to deconstruct and understand our lives as they are, and create what could be.

Having students imagine the future is a great way to help them develop their digital citizenship skills. The goal isn't to convince students to produce less technology. Nor is it to have them produce more. The goal is to help them think about innovation in ways that are more human-centric and goal driven. This activity allows them to see "the medium" of technology, to imagine new futures, to understand how new technologies might connect and disconnect us, and ultimately to consider how they can blend their digital lives and real lives creatively and proactively. In the advanced version of this exercise, we also consider other drivers of technological innovation, including Dertouzos' theory of "the ancient human," the narrative arc of innovation, and McLuhan's *Four Laws of Media*. But those considerations are for another time.

That's probably enough for one sitting. But before we go, let me share an idea with you about a technology I would like to create. I call it the Revealer. It looks like a reverse megaphone. That is, you speak into the large end, and listen through the small opening on the other end. Its unique capability is its ability to translate whatever you say into what you actually mean. So, imagine your IT director denies your request for an iPad because he is afraid everyone will want one. What might emerge from the small end of The Revealer is something like, "As a child, all I ever wanted was a dog and my parents wouldn't let me have one." You might get a similar result when your boss responds to your questions about why you can't use the coffee pot in the executive area, or when your partner tells you that you need to change your hairstyle to update your brand. Imagine the depth that The Revealer could bring to otherwise innocuous conversations about the weather. Or how handy it could be at strategic planning retreats or family reunions. We could really get to the bottom of some long standing issues. Who wants to crowdsource The Revealer with me? You may be shy about this now, but you'll see. It will be an app in no time.

Whether you leave committed to buying my Revealer app or not, I hope this thought is firmly embedded in your mind: Technology connects and disconnects, and the fully educated person wants to have a proactive sense of how this happens. Please ask questions about how to mitigate the disconnections and always seek to have technology amplify what's best in humanity. Talk with each other, our students and your children about being digital citizens and the lives we all lead online. Be sure to provide them opportunities to flex their ethical muscles by letting them help make the rules. Above all, talk to them about the story they want to tell about themselves on the great stage of the Internet, and help them become the people they want the rest of the world to know.

And whatever you do, please go tell your story.

Thank you.

IDEA **3**

FIVE TRENDS THAT BEND

Technological Trajectories that will Change Everything

Pimp Your Mind

I have a lot of ground to cover this morning so I'm going to go like a roller coaster without brakes. If you want to follow up with me afterwards you can find me through my name: jasonOhler.com, @gmail, @Twitter, @LinkedIn and all of those social media networks that won't leave me alone. But be careful. There are quite a few Jason Ohlers out there. One seems to have quite a gun collection. That's not me. Another has auto mechanic skills I wish I had. That's not me either. Another is having a land dispute with the federal government. I wish him well with his struggles. Of course, in order to distinguish among us you would need to care about the truth, and you would have to commit to doing the research necessary to discover what the truth actually is. And who has time to do that? We, the time challenged, live in a world of the somewhat credible, in which connectivity often substitutes for knowledge, and instantaneous revisionist history and personal bias form the foundation of our narrative. When a Google search yields millions of hits in under a second, what's a busy person to do?

To make sure you have the right me, you can go to jasonohler. com, where you can download this presentation. As you can see, I own the version of Photoshop with the biceps option. It's so much easier than actually exercising. Well, who's got time to do that, either? Not having time. This is a recurring theme in this  presentation. We are info overwhelmed and time squeezed. More about this aspect of the modern condition as the presentation progresses.

Now, I realize that having a demanding schedule is no excuse for ignoring the impacts of entropy on my body as I slide into my sunset years. That's certainly the litany espoused by infomercial exercise evangelists. But the reality is that I am much more concerned about how the aging process will damage my mental faculties. Fortunately, researchers at Vanderbilt University's Visual Cognitive Neuroscience Laboratory have developed a "neural enhancing cap" that boosts learning and improves decision-making by stimulating the brain's medial-frontal cortex. It apparently restores vigor and clarity to the thinking process. If I am worried about losing my spiritual edge, another kind of headware, dubbed the "god helmet," can replicate an out-of-body experience and simulate a feeling of metaphysical euphoria. At long last, the field of theology gets a learning lab. Other neuro-technologies that are being developed will increase our creativity and empathy, while still others will allow us to control objects, drive our cars, and interface with virtual reality. Mindfulness will get a technological boost.

However, one neuro-enhancing development should be of particular interest to us because it will turn education and the work place on its head. I often refer to the headware shown here as "the math hat" because apparently wearing it can improve our mathematical aptitude. Here's the question. If your kids' math scores could go up by 10% just by wearing a hat like this, would you buy it for them? Sure it's ugly, but we'll hire Apple to redesign it. Let's say it only costs $50–would you get it? In fact, one of the "trends that bend" that will become part of my presentation at some point will

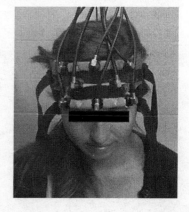

certainly be neuro and biological enhancement. Technologies will become available that will generate news stories like these:

- Math Hat Helps Students Pass Standardized Tests
- Parents Claim Unfair Advantage for Students Who Can Afford Advanced Neuro-stimulators
- Businesses Require Employees to Use Neuro-enhancers on the Job to Boost Productivity – Employees claim it is an infringement of their civil rights

These kinds of developments make us uncomfortable, largely because we feel powerless to stop them regardless of what we might think about them. Our free will, so it seems, has been hijacked by our innovative imperative. New technologies begin as unexpected conveniences, become necessities, and then morph into entitlements that we take for granted. Thereafter they become invisible, blending into the landscape as though they were always there. This adoption process seems to be our natural state.

Our dance with the cell phone in the workplace provides a good case in point. Back in the day, using our cell phones at work was grounds for dismissal. We were contractually required to use only the phones that were provided on site that were tethered to the wall by wires and made universally institutionalized beeping sounds when someone called us. Clients needed to contact us solely during "the work day"; business stopped at 5 PM. Fast forward to now, when most companies and organizations expect us to carry our personal devices with us at all times so that clients and customers can reach us whenever they need to. Some organizations may provide you with a cell phone, but then you have to deal with the thorny issue of determining which phone to use when someone calls with whom you have both a personal and business relationship. Besides, do you really want to carry two

115

phones around with you? Simply using our own phones has become the much easier option.

A similar change in attitude toward using our cell phones also happened on a more personal level. Do you remember during the early days of cell phones, when a few of your friends had them and you didn't? As you were sitting having coffee they would respond to a phone beep like Pavlov's dog, say something dismissive like "I gotta' take this" and leave you to float in a disconnected ether on the other side of the table, feeling some combination of disgusted, disappointed and insulted. Our collective attitude has flipped 180 degrees. In the spirit of "if you can't beat 'em, join 'em," we all purchased cell phones. Now we consider it irresponsible and unfriendly not to encourage our friends to take a call. After all, that's what we hope they would do for us. Besides, now that we are plugged in 24/7 we can always text (or call someone or play games or practice our French) while we wait for them to finish their business. The point is that our shift in attitude toward the mobile phone is indicative of what is about to happen with regard to all the new technologies that are destined to become part of our lives. At first we may distrust or dislike them, but then we will tolerate them, accept them and ultimately depend on each other to use them.

The technologies I have mentioned are not that far off. We need to remind ourselves that the future goes on for a very long time, with or without us, and that the world of exponential innovation is just getting started. Our futures will be filled with innovation because we don't ask why we should adopt new technologies, but rather why not. Our mantra is, "Because we can, we do, unless you can show me an overwhelming reason not to." This attitude is not unlike the one expressed by Edmund Hillary, the first to scale Mt. Everest, who did so simply "Because it's there." Why wouldn't we get our kids math hats given "they are there?" Park that question in the back of your mind for now. We'll get back to it.

Also park this observation attributed to McLuhan in the back of your mind. It defines the very essence of our relationship with emerging technology: "We shape our tools and thereafter they shape us." On the surface, cell phone adoption shaped a solution to a particular communication problem. However, just below the surface there unfolded a vast network of unintended consequences that began shaping us in the cell phone's image. Anytime, anywhere, communication technology created entirely new social structures and group dynamics. Adhocracies and dispersed corporations have arisen quite naturally as a result. Personal and private lives have blurred. "Time off" from work, parenting or socializing has become nearly impossible. The bottom line is that every new technology is a Pandora's Box, filled with unexpected consequences as well as hope for the future. Our only way to maintain a sense of stewardship about our technological future is to innovate consciously, and to inform our forward motion by what we see in the rearview mirror.

The Saga of the Info Overwhelmed

But I'm getting ahead of myself. I'm really here to tell you a story. It's a tale about being overwhelmed by information and digital opportunity, and five technological trends that both cause and solve the problems that come with living an advanced technological lifestyle. The first trend I'm going to talk about is *Big Data*. It addresses the question, "What happens when we have the capacity to collect, store and process all the information we want?" Big Data presents the same kinds of problems and opportunities that we would experience if we had an infinitely large attic. The second trend we will look at is *Immersive Reality*, or IR. Our new normal is that we all live in two places at once, in RL, or real life, and in IR, the immersive reality on the other end of our smart devices that surrounds us with data wherever we go. Our story will focus on one particular expression of how we bring our two worlds together, augmented reality (AR). The third trend we will consider is *The Semantic Web*, which consists of two parts: Web 3 - the Internet of data, and Web 4 - the Internet of things, or IoT. They are merging into what is often referred to as the "Internet of Everything," or IoE. Regardless of how we deconstruct it, The Semantic Web will change us profoundly in many ways.

The fourth trend is our rapidly advancing *Bring Your Own Device* or BYOD culture, in which we carry our immersive, interconnected, technologically amplified lives with us wherever we go. In particular, we'll be interested in some of the technologies on the extreme edges of BYOD, much of which is wearable and inconspicuous. Of course, whatever is extreme today will be normal tomorrow. And finally, the fifth trend we will consider is *Transmedia Storytelling*–telling stories and presenting information across all the "now media" of the day, from books to Facebook, from instant messages to Instagram, to whatever media is next that we can't even imagine. Transmedia storytelling is huge in business, organizational planning, branding and just about everywhere but education. At least for now. Keep in mind that each one of these trends is worthy of a weeklong TED talk. My purpose here is to help make some basic sense of how these trends affect our lives as we head into a future that is coming at us with unbelievable velocity.

This is the hero of our story. She's obviously having a bad day. Why? Because she is so overwhelmed with information she doesn't know what to do. She represents all of us. She is our "every person," our average digitally deluged human being who questions whether having too much information and technological opportunity today is better than having too little not long ago. She can't quite shake her nostalgia for the days when the school library's encyclopedia was her main source of information. She remembers her heart racing as she ran to the library to be the first to grab the "N volume" after her teacher announced that a report on Napoleon would be due in three days. She can close her eyes and feel the heft of an encyclopedia volume in her hands, and remember the musty smell of knowledge that wafted from its pages. Despite her visceral attachment to the past, she knows that nostalgia is simply an irrational longing for limitations she can no longer afford. She knows she needs to upgrade her mindset and her skills in order to deal with all of the information and opportunity in her life. It is her acknowledgement of this challenge that makes the journey possible.

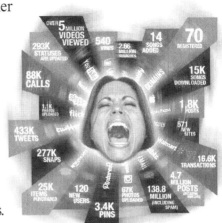

The reality for all of us is that data overload is the elephant in the room that we rarely acknowledge. But what can we say about it? We can't avoid it or stop it from growing. So, we get used to it as it forms an invisible, secondary ecology that eludes our conscious detection. One reason we do not complain about our situation may be the small shot of dopamine we apparently receive every time we get a text message or an email. We may well be on a pleasure high all day long as we unwrap the data gifts that arrive in our in-baskets, even though we can't intelligently process a fraction of them. While we wait for science to confirm this, it is easy to connect this possibility with the focus (some would say addiction) we exhibit when engaging with our smart devices.

How much information are we swimming in these days? Our hero hasn't done the math yet, so let me provide a personal perspective. I asked myself recently, "How much time would be required for me to responsibly process the information I receive in an average day?" I'm not talking about just scanning headlines, hoping that magically I might be able to discern which might lead to news that is truly important. I am talking about actually reading or watching what I receive, following a link or two within the text, thinking a bit about what I explored and maybe joining the conversation to some small degree. How much time would it take to do this?

Before I respond, let me tell you about my typical data intake. I subscribe to seven or eight mail lists, and scads of newsletters and blogs. I'm sure you all do. Why not? They're free! I belong to a number of on-going conversations with people in my profession. I receive many recommendations to watch TED Talks, read books and visit websites that appear to be essential to my professional development if I want to be up to date in my field. We're all in the same boat. Now, I can always turn off the spigot. But, like you, I don't. Much of what comes my way is relevant to my interests, and it seems irresponsible to ignore it.

So, how much time would it take to respond responsibly to all of this? My back-of-the-napkin calculation estimates that it would take about a month, and that would require skipping work, lunch, walking the dog, taking power naps and playing with my grandkids. If I don't skip these activities then I would need about two months. To be clear, it would take me about two months to process a day's worth of information, and that's only if I don't pay attention to forwarded blog posts like this one from a Huffington Post feed: "33 Can't-Miss New Books You'll Want to Curl up with This Fall." If I wanted to follow up on recommendations like this, then I would need an army of coordinated clones working around the clock to help me keep up.

The hero of our story concurs. She, like the rest of us, finds herself in a most amazing situation: Information abundance has become disruptive, and she doesn't know what to do about it. She doesn't really have anything to compare it to. Having an information surplus isn't like having too much food. After all, whatever we don't eat today can become tomorrow's leftovers. However, it's worth pointing out that we're usually amazed by what we find when we do get around to cleaning out the refrigerator once a year. Most things in plastic containers look like biology projects.

The difference between food and information is that the latter has a much shorter shelf life. Even though information can sit in a file indefinitely, we rarely have time to return to it. Most of it needs to be processed right now because we will need to use our limited attention resources to process the new information that will arrive any moment to replace it. The info smorgasbord keeps expanding, but we can only eat so much. We can always go on a diet by adopting information filters, but what's the most nutritional information out there? In large part, our hero's journey is all about the quest to find vitamins for the mind that are digestible, healthy and essential.

We will follow our hero through her narrative arc, which can be simply described as follows: *The journey that our hero takes through the "trends that bend" transforms her from someone who is paralyzed by the information and innovation in her life to someone who understands how to better manage information abundance in personal, meaningful ways. As a result, she falls cautiously in love with a world of ever expanding information and technological possibilities, ever vigilant of their limitations.* In this story she will undergo the hero's transformation on her journey by learning how to navigate the waters of disruptive abundance. She will emerge victorious, if not a bit tired. Given that her story is also our story, we gladly take this journey with her. We will learn, as she learns, how to find a path with a heart in a world of excessive opportunity. To be honest, I'm not seeing big name actors vying to play the lead. But this could be just the right story for an indie film production.

If you will permit me, I will be her guide. It is up to me to lead the way, to explain various mileposts during our journey. I will help her hack her way through the ever expanding data thickets of the web, and stay afloat in the oceans of continually emerging innovation and possibility. We will check in with our hero as the story progresses so that we can understand her perceptions of the journey and what she is learning from her quest.

During our travels we will look at the "trends that bend" in terms of how they challenge her and help her, as well as how they impact education and society. We will also look at them through the lens of digital citizenship, a topic I explore in depth in another presentation. For now, all we need to know about digital citizenship is that it provides a "big picture" perspective that encourages us to see the technology and information opportunities in our lives in terms of how they connect and disconnects us. Connections are easy to see because typically they are shiny, exciting and immediate. In contrast, disconnections are often difficult to detect because they are subtle, unintended and gradual. The goal is to see both so that we can balance innovation's opportunities and limitations.

As we travel with our hero through the five trends that bend, let's keep a fundamental question in the forefront of our minds. It should guide everything we do. Put simply the question is: *"What do we want?"*

We are living in an era that is immensely and collectively creative. We occupy a vast art studio called the Internet that allows us to look over each other's shoulders and feed each other's need for ideas, resources and inspiration. As a result, the gap between our imaginations and our productivity is becoming shorter all the time. Now that we can create whatever we want, we need to address the question, "What do we want?" This question used to have all the reality of asking how many angels fit on the head of a pin. These days, answering this question has become quite pressing. We should ask this question about our educational systems, our societies and our personal lives. In a world in which millions of programmers can create apps that astound us; medical engineers can print new body parts and create nanobots that can cure what ails us; and scientists can fashion the materials we dig out of the ground into just about anything, we can have whatever we want. So, *what do we want?*

Trend One: Big Data

As we head out on our journey, I explain to our hero that the reason we're looking at a picture of a 737 engine is because in December of 2012 there was a 737 Alaska Airlines flight en route from Seattle to Anchorage that had to make an emergency landing in Juneau. Everything had been going fine until the unthinkable happened: One of the engines stopped working. This is the kind of incident  that rattles anyone who flies with any frequency. Our hero has experienced a few disconcerting moments in a plane and can easily imagine the panic the passengers must have felt as they waited for the plane to land safely at the Juneau airport. She wants to know what happened, which, as you will see, provides an effective segue into the world of Big Data.

I travel a good deal on Alaska Airlines' 737s, which inspired me to set up a Google Alert for "737 failure" to look for clues. Much to my dismay, in the next four months I received three alerts about 737 engine failures that had been experienced by other airlines elsewhere in the world. I wondered to myself, "Is anybody looking into this?"

I decided to investigate and a month later had a phone meeting with a representative from the FAA. The man I spoke with was so friendly and knowledgeable that he restored my faith in the saying, "I'm from the government and I'm here to help you." In so many words he said, "I hope it makes you feel better to know that before that plane landed in Juneau, I was at a table in Seattle with representatives from GE who made the engine, Boeing who bought it, Alaska Airlines who used it and our folks from the FAA, and we had already figured out the problem and designed a fix for it." Their quick problem solving was made possible by the fact that the flight in question generated two terabytes of flight data that was streamed to a data analysis hub on the ground. The information SWAT team that had gathered around the table had analyzed the data using specialized software that pinpointed the issue in short order. I got the impression that this was just a normal day's work for them. It's important to note that live streaming and recording flight information is not standard operating procedure for all airlines, largely due to cost rather than technological capability. However, smart airlines use this technology or are making moves to do so because of the obvious improvements it offers over Black Box recorders. One day it will become standard practice.

Feel free to be amazed by the fact that a plane can generate and stream two terabytes of data, which is actually a small amount of data given the average airliner's current capabilities. However, I prefer you be amazed by the fact that we no longer have data storage limitations, at least for now. Ten years ago two terabytes was a dream few could afford. Today it is the new normal. Keep in mind that the data I am talking about here is related to one relatively short flight, by one airline, on one day. As all airlines begin streaming data, one only needs to do some basic multiplication to imagine the mountains of data this will create. We haven't even considered all the recorded video feeds in the world, or the data that Facebook and Google collect about us on a moment-by-moment basis. We see massive data generation everywhere, not only on our desks and in the cloud, but also in the sky.

The youth in the audience are yawning. Two terabytes? Wake me up when you're talking about a zettabyte, which is a 1 followed by 21 zeroes. But it wasn't long ago that I saw a grown man in Costco openly weep because he could buy a two terabyte hard drive for $200. My first hard drive could store only ten megabytes of data and cost $1,000; so, I understood his emotional moment and nearly wept along with him. Incidentally, I recently purchased a five terabyte hard drive for around $100. I think I see a pattern.

I had the great pleasure of listening to Marshall McLuhan lecture at the University of Toronto during the 1970s, and the case of unlimited storage is a poignant example of how the medium is the message, or, as McLuhan sometimes preferred to call it, *the massage*. It wasn't long ago that we used to record camera feeds to VHS tapes. The tapes were bulky, expensive, and so limited in terms of storage capacity that we had to erase and reuse them frequently. The quality of the information they stored degraded with each recording, reducing their accuracy and long-range utility. As a medium, a VHS tape's message was "don't record much, don't record often, and don't expect quality." Tapes were replaced by CDs, then by several iterations of hard drives, and ultimately by today's technology that allows us to store an amount of data that was unthinkable a decade ago. And because we can, we do. As a result, we are the most recorded generation in history. While this development might bother us, it shouldn't surprise us. The human condition dictates that we innovate and then adapt to the new realities we create for ourselves. I doubt you'd ever throw anything away again if you suddenly had an infinitely large attic. The medium of the infinite attic would bring out your inner pack rat. Imagine a world without garage sales.

How Big Is Big? Consider a few numbers generated by Internet Live Stats during a twenty-three hour period on October 5, 2015:

- 849 million: number of Tweets tweeted
- 4.22 billion: number of Google searches conducted
- 210 billion: number of emails sent

More interesting and relevant to us are big data references like the following. According to a 2013 article, Google was processing over 20 petabytes of user-generated data a day; a petabyte is a 1 followed by 15 zeroes. I read that a petabyte of information would fill 20 million filing cabinets, though I have not personally verified that figure. According to a 2012 article, a report produced by Facebook claimed that it scanned 105 terabytes of data every 30 minutes. Presumably Facebook is looking for social interaction and consumer preference patterns, the heartbeat of social media consumer campaigns.

These companies are very upfront about the fact that they read our email and social media. Why do they do it? Supposedly to give us what we want: easy access to products and opportunities that are aligned with our interests. When we're communicating with friends about going to Hawaii, big data entrepreneurs can provide us with the latest deals on airplane tickets, and even flip flops and snorkeling gear, all without our asking. The ads that accompany our web searches or chitchat with friends appear because, according to big data think, we summoned them to appear. After all, this is what we want, isn't it, to have technology anticipate and fulfill our needs without our having to ask? We have a love-hate relationship with this kind of big data intrusion into our lives. We hate it as overbearing until we receive a notice about upcoming special rates at our favorite hotel, which we love to frequent because it provides an extended happy hour, heated pool facilities and free dance lessons. Suddenly spam becomes welcomed news.

Most importantly, we need to understand that in the universe of Big Data our output becomes Big Data's input. Burn this into your psyche: Our output is Big Data's input. This is how our arrangement with Big Data works. Another important takeaway is the fact that Big Data is not a big deal anymore. Big Data swirls around us like air. We've adapted to the fact that we feed its algorithms because in return we receive an unlimited supply of free apps and information, as well as a highly customized feedback loop that supposedly provides us a clearer view of who we really are and what we really want. We should also understand this: There is no separating ourselves from the Big Data juggernaut. We all want to be able to find out whatever we want about everyone else, as long as no one can find out whatever they want about us. However, our arrangement with Big Data doesn't work that way. Everyone else includes us. It is very much a package deal that allows analysts to distill and predict our behaviors, buying patterns, likes and dislikes. Their data points and analyses link broadly to our wider demographic and deeply to the individual profiles we have created through our past activities. Without these profiles we will never hear about the deals at our favorite hotel. Incidentally, it is worth noting that Big Data is "big" not only in terms of breadth, depth and magnitude, but also longevity. Recent advancements in optical storage assure data reliability for many years. The title of an *Engadget* online magazine article about this development tells the story: *'5D' discs can store data until well after the sun burns out.*

Big Data's 4 V's. Big Data researchers talk about the four qualities they seek in Big Data, often referred to as the 4 V's: volume, validity, veracity and velocity. What distinguishes these criteria from those used in previous research paradigms is velocity. Traditional research uses a static data set that has no velocity. Data is collected over a specific period of time that has a clear start and stop date about a specific group of people and events. For example, if we're going to study the results of a math intervention program being used in 9th grade, the parameters of the research project might consist of a particular class of 9th graders using particular math materials for a particular purpose during a particular school semester. Researchers frame their research, collect the data it generates and shut off the data spigot. If they don't, they risk their study leaking into everything. Then they hunker down to perform a lengthy analysis before producing usable results. Researchers have used this approach for many years to assess the viability of everything from educational materials to automobile advertising campaigns.

The world of Big Data uses a very different research paradigm. Big Data analysts don't want to turn off the data stream. They want to accumulate as much data as they can, as often as they can, from as many sources as possible. To big data infopreneurs, life consists of an endless stream of "micro-moments" that they analyze on the fly, allowing them to build their analyses cumulatively and longitudinally, nearly in real time. The lag time between activity and analysis is moving to zero.

Big Data analysis also differs from traditional research in another important way: subject consistency. In the example used above, researchers depend on the same 9th graders being involved throughout the study. Losing or adding subjects could compromise the integrity of the data. In contrast, Big Data research subjects are expected to come and go. They sign on to a media service, and sign off, often unpredictably; they are active one week, and not another; they leave one provider to join another for a better deal, while new users enter the media space on a regular basis. This is considered normal behavior within the social mediasphere.

Big Data uses a branch of mathematics to crunch data that is generically known as predictive analytics. This mathematical discipline has been with us for some time, but has never been as important as it is today. Fast computers and unlimited data storage are bringing a level of power to data analytics that was unthinkable a decade ago. All the data that researchers collect goes into the predictive analytics blender. This includes not only our demographics and credit card data, but also our conversations and blog posts. Powerful text analyzers evaluate our Facebook discussions and Tweets to determine a good deal about our personalities, characters and, most importantly, our buying behaviors, which is the holy grail of commercial information gathering. Literally anything from our digital footprints–all those bits and pieces of ourselves that we leave online wherever we go–can become part of a predictive analytics data set.

What's truly important to understand is this: Not only does our output become Big Data's input, but also Big Data's outputs then become our choices. Burn this into your psyche: Big Data's outputs become our choices. We have come full circle by creating a closed loop of inputs and outputs that provides the illusion of offering us free will. Those in the big data world read us, fashion our options, and almost imperceptibly create an intellectual and emotional space for us that social media activist Eli Pariser calls a "filter bubble." Another way to frame this is that we find ourselves reading what former director of MIT's Media Lab Nicholas Negroponte called the "daily me."

Our personal space is shaped by whatever big data purveyors bring to it commercially, socially and politically, which is guided of course by what they think we want according to the previous choices we have made. There is some truth to the idea that predictive analytics make us prisoners of our past.

What's in Your Bubble? Even though it's easy to blame Big Data for all of the information myopia in our lives, the reality is that our "bubbles" are also affected by our desire to see, understand and actively reprogram them.

Let's pause for a thought experiment. It is based on research I require my media psychology PhD students to conduct to help them better understand the personal bias they bring to their research perspectives. Briefly, I ask them to note the information sources they use over the course of a few days so that they can determine the biases and filters they have adopted by virtue of the information source choices they have made. I invite you to do the same. I assure my students that I'm not going to look at their information inventories because they sometimes find them embarrassing. I make you the same promise.

To carry out this activity, see yourself as a big data repository. Consider all of your information sources: newscasts, conversations with friends, blog readings, TED talks, TV shows, magazines you read in the checkout line at the supermarket but are too embarrassed to actually buy–whatever you turn to in order to feed your point of view. These information sources reflect choices you make among a myriad of options. So, what guides your choices?

If we conduct our information inventories honestly, and think deeply and objectively about what we discover, we are often forced to acknowledge this foundational concept of media psychology: we make up our minds about a topic *before* we have gathered information about it, not afterwards. Towards that end we apply information filters to our information input beforehand in order to limit what it is we will see. When we stumble upon facts or perspectives that fall outside our worldview then we find a way to make them fit, the way the Catholic Church made Galileo's heavenly observations fit a model of the universe that said the sun revolved around the earth. In practical, mundane terms this means that when we hear a statement by those we don't like–whether by politicians, celebrities, family members or colleagues–we listen for what we disagree with, or we find ways to interpret what we hear to conform to our previous view of them. We all want to believe we are rational researchers who are open to the truth. However, in the words of my theology teacher Father David Belyea, we are drops of reason in oceans of emotions. Our goal in using this approach to information selection and processing is to avoid the chaos that occurs when our worldview is threatened; when given the choice between survival and truth, we usually choose survival.

The bottom line is this: our most informed response to living in a world of Big Data is to cultivate our peripheral vision. In the world that I create in my novel, *Then What?,* there are freedom consultants who help clients with their information myopia, advising them on how to balance and broaden their perspectives. In the absence of freedom consultants, each of us needs to decide how to pursue a more balanced information and technology diet.

Big Data and Digital Citizenship. Now let's consider Big Data through the lens of digital citizenship and education. Two fairly recent news stories will help us address both.

I'm sure many of you have heard about the Facebook study in which researchers covertly fed positive and negative posts to two large groups of users in order to study their responses. How did Facebook justify not asking participants for their permission to be involved? By claiming users had already given it. Apparently, the fine print of the user agreement that we all accept but never read gives Facebook permission to conduct these kinds of activities. The researchers eventually produced an article titled, *Experimental Evidence of Massive-Scale Emotional Contagion through Social Networks.* Some of the 700,000 unsuspecting Facebook participants weren't very happy about having their emotions deliberately and secretly manipulated so that researchers could watch what happened. I don't know of anyone who was sued over the study, but we can still feel its aftershock. We want to know *Who* is watching us? *Who* is manipulating us? And, what do *They* want? Recalling that all technology connects and disconnects, the disconnect here is very clear.

Big Data is coming into its own in education, and we should be asking the same questions about how it is being applied to the world of teaching and learning. Anything that is connected to a network or enters the cloud potentially can be captured and become part of a Big Data profile. Data inventory specialists can collect keystrokes, text from chat rooms, test scores, choices made when playing games, you name it. All of these data sources can be accommodated by Big Data analytics.

On the surface, this offers great promise. Educational institutions can use Big Data to tailor learning materials and processes to the specific needs of each student. This approach is mainly based on the medical model. Patients wear wristbands so medical staff can track preferences, allergies and other personal characteristics in order to make sure patients use treatments that aren't harmful and have the best chance of succeeding. The Big Data adaptation in education is similar to this, minus the wristband–at least for now. Educators can review reports based on Big Data analyses, see that a student responds to hands-on manipulatives or gaming simulations, and personalize her learning to take advantage of those methodologies. The bottom line is that educational designers can build approaches to instruction based on the history and learning patterns that students have established for themselves.

That was certainly the thinking behind a collaborative effort lead by inBloom, The Gates Foundation, the Carnegie Corporation of New York and school districts from nine states when they converged on the creation of a centralized repository of K-12 student information that sought to collect data on millions of students. Parents were concerned because project managers didn't always seek permission to include student data, claiming permission was implied in the paperwork parents signed when their children started school. Parents' anxiety was exacerbated by the fact that their children's data was going to be offered to third-party vendors without clear reporting about who would have access to it or how it was going to be used. Another worry point was that the project provided the option of collecting very personal data, including information about learning disabilities, the nature of family relationships and even social security numbers. Ultimately the effort folded, largely because anxious parents couldn't get the reassurances they wanted about the safety of their children's information.

I'm not suggesting there was any impropriety on inBloom's part. That's not the point. A project like this could be very helpful in a world in which data is secure and managed only by honest, wise people. But in the imperfect world in which we live the downside is formidable. There have been enough news stories lately about hackers taking down data fortresses to convince us of the inherent vulnerabilities of our systems.

Would this project have collected data from social media sites as well? Probably not in its original design. However, adding this feature would not be very difficult to do. An enterprising third-party vendor could easily build a bridge between social media sites and a school database based on common data elements. Such a service would most certainly add another dimension of evaluation that many would be eager to have.

Balancing Big Data Isn't Easy. Big Data cuts both ways. It connects us to customer-driven, individualized education, while forcing us to live within an education filter bubble. Learning analytics equations prescribe possible student-centered pathways to success. However, they don't easily accommodate inspiration, drawing outside the lines, or the impacts of a gifted teacher on student development, which are some of the most compelling ingredients of student success.

Access to our data is another issue that cuts deeply in both directions. Providing access to information about our health, learning styles, and personal preferences can be extremely helpful. However, the same information can also brand us for life. Well-meaning employers who read about a student's learning disability might misinterpret it to mean that the student is incapable of performing a job. The student, who has long since grown up and overcome his disability or was misdiagnosed in the first place, is unable to defend himself because he doesn't know that such information about him exists. Even if he did know about it, updating it is very difficult; just ask anyone who has tried to convince a credit reporting company to fix an inaccurate credit report. The reality is that data is usually impossible to recall once it is in circulation. This means that profiles about us that are based on younger versions of ourselves who didn't know better at the time, or on information that was never the slightest bit true to begin with, can persist in the infosphere. While each of us wants to be understood, none of us wants to be profiled.

How does Big Data help our info-overwhelmed hero? By providing her a boat with a compass to help her to stay afloat as she navigates oceans of data. Without these, she would be absolutely and utterly lost. Drowning, in fact. Again, the issue is time. There simply isn't enough time to collect, coordinate, personally verify or make sense of the information in our lives. So, we turn to Big Data, which, like other sciences, exists to help us make sense of a complicated world.

But our hero remains suspicious of Big Data's motives

and has ideas about how to change the situation. Presently, data companies scoop up our information and use it for their purposes–largely to increase consumer engagement and product consumption. Our hero echoes a sentiment found in my book, *Then What?,* in which the book's hero offers an alternative: "What if we turned this around, and we could actually ask information companies to run a Big Data analysis for us that was driven by our goals, not theirs? What if we owned the information, and subcontracted them to take care of it and mine it for us?" Online advertising would probably come to a screeching halt. Or perhaps it would just be more user-directed. But imagine being able to ask Big Data companies to crunch our data to answer the question, "What am I missing?" rather than simply accepting that it is their job to skulk around in the background trying to second-guess what kind of shoes we want to buy. Imagine using Big Data analytics to help us broaden our perspective and see the real world more clearly. We might find we actually had more to say about how the big data juggernaut moved in and out of our lives. For now, our hero sees big data analytics as part of the solution to her info overwhelment issues but wants to ask Big Data to offer more user-directed services. She proceeds on her journey cautiously.

Trend Two: Immersion

As committed as our hero is to her journey of self-discovery, she needs to pause to read her emails, respond to her text messages and check her credit card activity for suspicious purchases. Twice last year her credit cards were hijacked, forcing her to go through the tedious process of cancelling her accounts and starting all over.

Living Two Places at Once. Like everyone else, she is immersed. Immersion is a term that has been largely co-opted by the entertainment industry to refer to technology-based experiences that combine physical and digital realities. However,

I use the term more broadly to describe the general state of being embedded in a secondary world of real-time information on the other end of our smart devices wherever we go. The new normal is that we live in two places at once, real life (RL) and immersive reality (IR). It is up

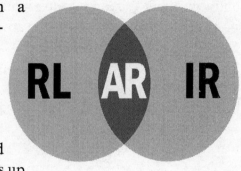

to each of us to combine these two realities into one integrated sense of place.

Much of our information "overwhelment" is caused by our need to manage and integrate our two realities. Our hero wonders whether life wouldn't simply be more manageable if she turned off her smart devices and re-entered RL full time. While this idea is very enticing, the reality is that leaving out half of her life would only increase her confusion. She would spend most of her time out of the loop wondering what was going on within it. We have heard of families who actually turn off their cell phones while eating dinner. They are the stuff of legend. The rest of us leave our devices on 24/7/365.

A good deal of innovation is now focused on technology that blends RL and IR. One such blend is augmented reality or AR, which I will focus on during this leg of our journey. Before I do, I want to mention a few others that are evolving rapidly and show great promise.

There is holography, which projects the appearance of people and objects into our RL environments. A good example is Princess Leia delivering her message to Luke Skywalker and Obi-Wan-Kenobi in the original *Star Wars* movie. Holography doesn't require goggles or personal smart devices. Instead, it uses projection devices that beam holographic images into our physical space.

There is also virtual reality, which takes us deep inside our minds and leaves us only minimally connected to RL. I'm sure you've seen the VR headware that looks like oversized ski goggles. What you might not have seen are the low-end goggles, like Google Cardboard, which allow you to turn your smart phone into a virtual reality experience. Affordable VR is inching its way into our lives.

There are also virtual worlds, like Second Life; gaming worlds, like Minecraft; and kinesthetic worlds, like those we experience with Wii and Kinect systems. Each combines our RL and IR differently. On the horizon are technologies like Magic Leap, which projects images directly on to the user's eye, and a number of wearable technologies, which I will address in Trend 4: xTreme BYOD.

However, I am going to focus on AR because it is well adapted to the mobile world, has gained a great deal of momentum and has come to users mostly free of charge. To use AR, I download a free or cheap app to my smart device and do a bit of low level programming that any English major can do–I started my academic career as an English major, by the way. Then, as I am walking down the street and use my phone to look at a restaurant across the street, voila, up comes the restaurant's list of lunch specials. There's no need to search the Net for the restaurant and then find the right button to click to see what's on the menu. Instead, the menu magically appears with very little effort. AR is a world of triggers and overlays. I look at the restaurant, which "triggers the overlay" to come down from the cloud; in this case the overlay is the menu that appears on our screen. This kind of magic can also occur using your iGlasses, whenever accessories like Google Glass come back into vogue. One day it will also occur using your contact lenses and connected clothing. And the future is just getting started.

Art Galleries and ARt Galleries. My wife, Terri, and I

created an augmented reality art gallery for K12 students–
an "ARt" gallery, as we like to call it. In many ways, the ARt
gallery was a conventional art gallery in that visitors wandered
among the exhibits and gazed at artwork that was displayed on
the walls. However, it was also a value-added gallery; looking at
the artwork through an AR-enabled device triggered an overlay
to come down from the cloud, combining both on the gallery
visitor's screen. The overlay might consist of more artwork that
was needed to finish what was hanging on the wall, in which
case the artwork was complete only when visitors were looking
at it with their devices. Or the overlay might be a video of
the artist explaining her artwork, or music that accompanied
the artwork. There are an unlimited number of ways to combine
triggers and overlays, particularly in the world of art.

This image is just one example of student work that the ARt
gallery featured. Here you see two self-portraits drawn by the
same student, Kate Karafotas, whose work was part of a grade

8 visual arts project
called *Inner Dialogue*
at the International
School of Prague. The
portrait on the left was
the trigger and the
only part of her work
that was physically
present in the gallery.
It represented how the

artist felt that others viewed her. The portrait on the right was
the overlay supplied by the Cloud and could only be seen by an
AR enabled smart device. It represented how she saw herself.
If it feels like we're living in The Matrix, that's because we are–
presumably in one of its very early versions. If I can look at a
wall, and see just a wall, and then look at the same wall through
my cell phone or my smart pad and see a painting, then I'm

in The Matrix. This is what AR allows us to do. Kate's work provided a poignant approach to using technology to explore concepts of personal identity.

My involvement in art and technology over the past three decades has led me to the following conclusion: I know only one thing for certain about the technology that awaits us in the future, and that is that we will find ways to use it to create art and tell stories. Our innate creativity demands it. Augmented reality art is a compelling example of our natural proclivities in this area. My involvement in art and technology has also lead me to another conclusion: If we don't use technology to create art, then technology will make art out of us. At that point, our humanity and our role in the stewardship of our innovative, digitally enhanced lifestyles will be in serious jeopardy. If we want humans rather than machines to direct the digital revolution, we will need artists to lead the charge.

AR can use a number of different kinds of triggers. One of these is location. The GPS in this woman's smart phone will enable her to receive information about the lighthouse she is visiting. Big Data keeps us at the center of the AR experience by personally tailoring the overlays we trigger on an individual basis. Her data profile "knows" that she sees herself as an historian first, and a botanist second, and will first  send her information about the history of the lighthouse before sending information about the nearby wildlife and plants. The AR experience can to be quite subjective in that regard.

AR can also be triggered by how we blink, how we move, and what we say. (As an aside, I asked my iPhone's Siri to tell me a joke the other day and it said, "The past, present and future walked into a room. It was tense." No joke.) I suspect one day AR will even be triggered by bio readouts, odors, ambient sounds, thoughts, and perhaps by the sensation of kissing. This is a picture of a kissing bot. No, your imagination is not playing tricks on you; the kissing bot does exactly what you are afraid to think it does. A user wraps his lips around a straw-like protrusion, someone on the other end of an Internet connection who is also using a kissing bot does the same, and they experience the sensation of kissing. We can only hope that they have a deep and lasting relationship. If this machine looks a little bit hokey, then just imagine version 3.0. It will certainly be AR-enabled, and perhaps provide tastes, odors and sounds. Actually, maybe it's better not to imagine version 3.0 of the kissing bot. Sometimes the future isn't for the squeamish.

Once you understand the basic idea behind AR–that you are immersed in a second world wherever you go, which you can access with your smart device to connect and blend two or more things, data points, places or experiences from RL and IR–then the world opens up. One of my university professors loved Robert Frost because he was a master of metaphor and of saying "this" in terms of "that." Think of AR as saying "this" in terms of "this and that." I warned you I was an English major.

There are a number of fascinating AR projects, many of which are well documented on YouTube. Business has embraced it in many ways. One application allows shoppers to try on clothes by standing in front of an AR mirror. This keeps them from making a trip to the changing room, and store personnel from having to pick up after them. Another application allows renters to see an empty room as a furnished office space, so they can determine whether it will meet their business needs before signing a lease. The medical community uses AR to show the inside of the human body for training purposes. Doctors use AR to merge X-rays on top of the human body to assist them during operations. Education has embraced AR in a number of ways. A shop teacher required his students to create an AR presentation that showed their understanding of the infrastructure behind the walls of a house. A group of science students tagged a wetlands area with AR markers so that visitors could receive instant information about whatever part of the ecosystem they were exploring.

I've actually been talking to some students in Alaska about creating an AR project for tourists. As tourists wander around town and visit an historical site, information about that site would come down from the Cloud and fill their smart screens. As they are walking past a clothing business, a message might appear like, "We're having a two for one sale on moose hats. Hurry!" How would a business get on the AR tourist walking tour? A small donation to the educational technology program at the students' school wouldn't hurt. AR is in its infancy. As of this writing, patents have been filed for AR projectors, as well as for devices that turn entire rooms into AR spaces without inhabitants needing to use special apps or gear. And the future is just getting started.

Where Might the Future Lead Us? I used to write a column called *Mining Movies* in which I speculated about how technologies that appeared in sci-fi movies might be used in education if they were actually developed one day. In many movies some form of AR was usually part of the technological landscape. In 1993, Oliver Stone's *Wild Palms* engaged us deeply in the world of AR visualization, much as we are starting to see it emerge today. In addition, the movie also transported us into a world of AR tactility, in which we could actually interact with elements of our AR world. This capability is currently under development. In the 2002 movie *Minority Report*, Tom Cruise looked pretty strange waving his arms around to manipulate images on his screen. Today, that technology simply looks like a more sophisticated version of Microsoft's Kinect. When these movies were made, very little of the technology that they featured actually existed. Now some of it is already on the market. I think we can see a trend here.

It was McLuhan who said that artists truly predict the future. Science fiction writers, who are free of all those pesky constraints like raising R&D capital and finding talent to actually make new technology, can afford to paint us an unfettered picture of our future possibilities. Movicians–movie makers who elevate movie making to an art form–give voice to the writers' visions. The future may just be getting started, but more importantly, how we imagine the future is just getting started as well. If we look to our artists, we will get a glimpse of where we are headed.

Now let's consider AR's educational implications, and also look at its connections and disconnections as digital citizens. I've already described some of the connections. The disconnections are less obvious. In an AR-enabled world, the world can read you. You can become a trigger. Who will control the overlay and the kinds of data they will provide? Will they include health, marital and work information? In a perfect world, where each of us can control our level of privacy, this isn't a problem. But we know better. The connections that others make for us, so that we can access their AR enabled world, will always present a challenge in terms of authenticity, accuracy and privacy. Also, distraction takes a quantum leap with AR. Checking your smart phone in the middle of an RL conversation is nothing compared to looking into a room and seeing people and things that literally aren't there. YouTube hosts a variety of truly funny videos about AR-enabled dating that give us a glimpse into how distracting and difficult it might be to live in two places at once.

How does AR help our info-inundated hero? She sees it as providing a possible antidote to spam and other unwanted data intrusions because it brings together two or more things, places or pieces of information that have a guaranteed connection. The result is directly relevant to us because, for the most part, we drive the connection. In this way, AR can be used as a very effective filtering tool to imagine information opportunity, and to use our ever dwindling time supply more effectively. Our hero can choose to manage her own immersive reality by creating her own AR connections, or she can act as a gatekeeper as she walks through other people's AR enabled worlds. This level of control contrasts with the world of Big Data, in which she never really knows what is going on. For now, our hero sees immersive reality as more of a friend than an adversary. Our hero continues her journey through the five "trends that bend," somewhat optimistic about where it is taking her.

Trend Three: The Semantic Web

To prepare for her journey through this trend, our hero performs a simple web search for herself. She finds much more than she feels comfortable sharing, including references to her volunteer work at a local homeless shelter (for which she would prefer not to be recognized because of her religious beliefs about performing anonymous acts of charity); social media postings that included videos of her singing karaoke off-key (she was forgiven, given it was her birthday and she was attempting an early Billy Joel song); and remote video feeds of her property so she can monitor activity when she is traveling (a password is required, but how hard would it be to figure it out or bypass it altogether?). Her monitoring system is intelligent enough to automatically contact her security company if intruders appear on her property. She bought the Pro version for an extra $49.95 a month, which includes the automatic employment of facial recognition software to cross-reference the identities of intruders with a database of "friendlies." If anyone is not in the database, the system calls the police department. This means that the Easter Seals volunteer who shows up at her door looking for a charitable contribution may need to explain her presence to the local sheriff. One day the Semantic Web will connect everything–our information, our things, our bodies, and even our thoughts. Everything connected by the Semantic Web will be searchable, cross-referenceable and capable of speaking to each other. The Semantic Web will be able to simulate intelligence well enough to make decisions without our direct involvement. And the Semantic Web is just getting started.

The Web Gets a New Foundation. The Semantic web is a drastically updated version of the Web we have experienced over the past twenty years. It is gradually coming online, and will eventually dominate the substructure of our experience on the Internet.

Someone's creating a new Web? Why didn't we get the memo?

We need to understand that the Web has already been rewritten many times, by all of us, as standards have changed and Web capacity and tools have been upgraded. The Web changes the way our body changes, shedding old layers and regenerating itself so gradually and so far below the surface that we don't notice. We just adapt to the new reality as it comes online, often unconsciously.

Where did the Semantic Web come from? Back in the Neolithic period of computer networking, circa 1960 to 1990, mainframes talked to mainframes, often using modems and the phone system. Average folks like myself and other English majors could dial into mainframes but could do very little beyond using email and playing with programming languages and statistical packages. Graphics and social media as we know them today were nowhere in sight. Basically, the techies ruled the machines and controlled much of the Web's content.

This is the communication architecture that was in place when Tim Berners-Lee created the initial Web; in hindsight, we'll call it Web 1.0. As of Web 1.0, anyone–even English majors–could contribute to the development of the Web who was willing to learn how to navigate its arcane passageways and develop the rudimentary programming skills necessary to create simple web pages. Most importantly, as of Web 1.0 everyone could enter the conversation about what the Web could become.

Web 1.0 morphed into Web 2.0, the world of blogs, wikis, social media and easy-to-make personal websites. Instead of having to write code, "websters" simply used templates; for most of us that meant that programming moved into the background where we didn't have to deal with it. Then came Web 2.1, a term that apparently only I use to describe what happened when multimedia was added to the Internet. The move from text-centric communication to the media collage opened up a cornucopia of expression. Because the Web was destined to be everywhere and provide a de facto standard for communication, literacy moved beyond letters and numbers (the 3Rs) to embrace the audio-visual domain (the 4Rs) on a grand scale. At that point art truly became the 4th R in a modern, digital-age sense.

That brings us to the Semantic Web. Currently, the Semantic Web consists of two major components: Web 3, or the Web of Data, which is primarily the world of IR; and Web 4, the Web of Things, which is primarily the world RL. They are rapidly merging into the "Internet of Everything," or IoE. However, I will address Webs 3 and 4 separately to help facilitate discussion about the role each plays in creating a unified immersive reality. I will begin with some Web 3 foundations.

Recall that Web 1.0 connected mainframes, while Web 2.0 connected web pages. Web 3 connects very specific pieces of data on specific websites. Web 3 is reportedly more along the lines of what Tim Berners-Lee originally envisioned when he created the Web. However, the public adopted his initial creation so quickly that there wasn't enough time to develop its semantic capabilities. He has been championing the development of the Web's semantic potential ever since.

Consider the advances in searching that Web 3 makes possible. A Web 2 search requires searching for a word or a phrase, much like we search for text in a word processing document. The search engine scours the Web looking for that text, and produces upwards of a gazillion hits. We are left to do the grunt work of slogging through the findings. This is still how most searching is conducted today. Incidentally, I was around when the public Web went live. I remember searching for the word "education" and receiving seven hits. That should impress you with how far the Web has come and how old I must be.

One of the results of Web 3 being connected at the data level (vs. just at the page level) is that it provides much smarter searching and even behaves as if it understands the intent of our search. By using data with established relationships, it can provide context and meaning to a search and, as a result, produce findings we didn't even know we were looking for. The bottom line is that Web 3's intelligent searching makes the linguistically messy business of human communication more digestible to machines, so that machines can make deeper and more meaningful information connections for humans.

Semantic searching is currently in limited use today. As of this writing you will see a combination of traditional and semantic search results when looking for information about, for example, "Michael Jackson." On the left hand side of the screen appear the Web 2.0 results, which consist of many thousands of discrete hits. What do we all do? If we are seriously interested in researching the topic then we get out our shovels and start digging. However, most of us are just casual searchers and will follow only the first page of results. This is why we all want our websites appear on the first page of Google search findings. Few people go any further than that.

On the right hand side of the screen appear the Web 3 search results. They look like a Wikipedia article–formatted, synthesized and organized. They are built on assumptions about what Web 3 thinks we want to know about Michael Jackson. Those assumptions are based on previous searches conducted by others as well as ourselves that were related to the topic of Michael Jackson. A semantic search is also facilitated by the common coding structure used to represent semantic data, which enables Web 3 to connect information from different sites, compile it and present it as a report. Reports are just the first stop in terms of presentation. As Web 3's sophistication grows, so will the output it produces. It will include graphs, infographics, perhaps even videos.

We are in the very early stages of Web 3. It works very well for the worlds of science and medicine, in which information is clearly structured. It doesn't work as well for the worlds of prose and chat, in which communication is difficult to categorize because it lacks inherent organization. Semantic Web developers are hard at work imbuing Web 3 with the ability to deconstruct text, and to code web data so that it is more machine friendly. One day we will look at Web 2.0 search results and chuckle, the way we chuckle when we see a floppy disk today.

Web 4- The Internet of Things. Now that we've explored Web 3, let's look at Web 4, the Internet of things. Through the use of tags, GPS technology, sensors and transmitters, all of which are becoming smaller and more discreet with each iteration, the things in our lives will have the ability to be connected to each other one day whether we feel they need to be or not. They will use the Internet as a kind of commons and will be capable of having a collegial relationship with each other, as well as with us.

Connecting smart devices to the things in our lives is fairly standard these days. We can already control our home and security systems remotely through our phones. We can see where our "chipped pets" are at all times. Some cities have smart parking meters that will tell our smart phones the best place to park and then monitor the time we have left. We can even give the system permission to charge our credit cards if it looks like we are running out of time. There are numerous examples of "phone-to-thing" communication like these.

However, things talking to "non-phone" things is a rather new development. Consider some of the objects you have with you at the moment other than your phone, like your pen and your shirt. One day they will routinely talk to each other. We are compelled to ask: What conversation would my pen and my shirt possibly want to have with each other, or with me? Just a bit of imagination can produce the following scenarios. Perhaps my pen has a leak that I hadn't noticed. I then receive an alert via my smart device to take care of it quickly before the stain sets on my shirt. Perhaps my pen is also one of the "surface sensing" styluses currently under development that allows me to acquire the color of a surface simply by tapping it, functioning much like an eyedropper tool in a digital photo retouching program. If I were wearing a "chameleon shirt" that can change colors as directed, which will no doubt exist one day, I could transfer the color of an unaffected part of my shirt to the section that had been stained; or, perhaps change my shirt to match the stain. Even more exciting, perhaps my tie is one of the new chameleon ties that can be reprogrammed to change color and pattern. I touch my pen on my shirt and then my tie, and wait for my artificial intelligence "fashionista" program to tell me whether they match. Or perhaps I transfer new colors and patterns that I find in my immediate environment to my tie until my artificial intelligence program tells me I'm perfectly coordinated with my surroundings.

If I were a politician, maybe I would elect to change my shirt and tie color throughout the day, depending on whom I was addressing and the image I wanted to project. In order to better identify with the locals, I might wear a checkered flannel shirt and a tie provided by the local chamber of commerce when I appeared at a hardware store. Later that day I might need to wear a powder blue button-down shirt and red power tie at a gathering of business leaders in order to project authority and economic confidence. I predict that one day we will see a fashion line called Spin wear, or perhaps Spinware. Capabilities like these seem like gratuitous overkill now. However, at one time so did being able to carry your phone with you wherever you went, or using a machine to wash your clothes, or receiving a lung transplant.

As more things become connected, the possibility for conversations among them will expand, regardless of how trivial these conversations might seem to us now. If we are looking for inspiration, Johnny Walker connected a number of bottles of its finest to the Internet through smart labeling, which enabled tracking the bottles across the supply chain, from manufacturing to consumption. Consumers who scanned the bottles with mobile devices received personalized, branded information about the product. Clever entrepreneurs will figure out how to sell us services like this, which connect all of our things in ways that are irresistible to us. A primary frontier in this regard is the smart home, which is being developed by a number of companies, including Apple via its HomeKit, a development platform that allows users to connect home devices and control them via Siri. The smart home raises the possibility of asking our cookbook to talk to our refrigerator and pantry, to determine whether everything needed for a recipe is on hand. A value-added smart home might be able to check the inventory at a local store to see whether it has whatever we're missing. If it does, and if time is tight (after all, company is due in an hour, and we still have to clean up), then perhaps our local store and Uber have an agreement that allows Uber to deliver the ingredients to our door. All of this comes at a cost, but it saves us our most precious commodity: time.

The connected world gets even more interesting when things talk to things, then talk to us–or perhaps not. For example, your car could sense there's a nail in your tire, which is causing low tire pressure. It finds the nearest gas station that has the right tires in stock, consults Google maps about the fastest way to get there, and then lets you know what it has decided. If you have a self-driving car, maybe it just begins its journey on its own and informs you en route. You can object, but why would you? Your tire is damaged. Better not risk an accident. After all, accidents can cost a lot of time.

Everything is Connected, Even Us. Through advancements in programming, the materials sciences, sensing and transmission technolgies, connectivity will be built into everything. We have evolved from a world in which nothing human-made was connected to one in which everything we make is connected. This includes whatever we type and speak, as well as whatever we make and use. After spending the past two decades swimming in a sea of 0's and 1s in our minds, we are coming home to the tactile world of RL. However, now it is a value added home that leverages our most precious commodity: time. We let our machines do more of the work so we have more time to... well, work, I guess. After all, someone has to pay for all of this.

Eventually everything is going to have some kind of web address, including life forms. Way back in 2010, geneticist and entrepreneur Craig Venter claimed to have created the first artificial life form. The following is an excerpt from a TED talk in which he announced his discovery:

> We're here today to announce the first synthetic cell. A cell made by starting with the digital code in the computer, building the chromosome from 4 bottles of chemicals, assembling that chromosome in yeast, transplanting it into a recipient bacterial cell and transforming that cell into a new bacterial species. This is the first self-replicating species that we've had on the planet whose parent is a computer. It also is the first species to have its own website encoded in its genetic code.

No big deal. Just making new life forms. It's fair to assume that this field has advanced markedly since 2010.

Could his discovery lead to actually making people? Most certainly, given that the future is just getting started. But seeing as how we will be engineering people from scratch in the laboratory, perhaps what's coming aren't people, but super people who are designed to compensate for whatever naturally occurring imperfections nature had in store for us at birth. When science develops this capability, we will see news stories like, "Child sues parents for not making him better looking and more athletic," and "Separate gifted and talented programs established for genetically enhanced children. Parents of non-enhanced children scream foul play."

Venters' work highlights the creation side of the DNA revolution. On the data analysis side we can predict our possible futures by understanding our DNA profiles. For example, science can identify genetic markers for a number of biological proclivities, including diseases. Use of this information will also lead to perplexing headlines. A *WIRED* news article recently reported that a middle school student was forced to leave school because he had the genetic marker for cystic fibrosis and could not be in the proximity of other children already attending the school who suffered from the same disease. Apparently the risk of mutual infection is too great. Even though this student hadn't developed cystic fibrosis, he was excused as a precautionary measure simply because he had the genetic marker for it. His parents are suing based on "genetic discrimination." This legal challenge is only one of the truly newsworthy stories here. The other is that a child was effectively being found guilty for something that hadn't happened yet. Forget the pre-cogs floating in the wading pool in *Minority Report*. We will use data analytics to replace the past with probable futures.

It is easy to extrapolate from this scenario. Imagine you are an HR director who is considering two candidates for a position. On the surface, Candidates A and B are equivalent: each has five years of experience, a great education, and comes with convincing letters of recommendation. However, Candidate B has the genetic marker believed to be associated with alcoholism. Such a genetic link is currently in dispute in the research community. However, whether or not the link is scientifically sound won't matter. And the fact that Candidate B can prove he has never had a drink in his life won't matter either. The specter of alcoholism will be deterrent enough to tip the scales toward Candidate A. Fear of litigation will drive the HR director's decision; should alcohol ever play a role in Candidate B's work performance, auditors will hold the HR department responsible for not hiring the "safer" candidate. This scenario applies to genetic discoveries related to depression, cancer and anything that might cost a company time, money or productivity. We live with the burden of knowing more than we can ethically process. Our knowledge will go toe-to-toe with civil rights in a digitally and biologically enhanced world. Will companies and schools begin requiring DNA profiles? Not tomorrow. But someday. As with our credit reports, we may actually want to publicize our profiles to show that we are free and clear of anything that might concern others.

Creepy, eh? I'm afraid it's all too possible. The Semantic Web will soon connect our data in ways that may inspire and frighten us. Regardless of how we feel about it, escaping its reach won't be an option. We should enjoy our genetic anonymity while we can. We should also enjoy this brief period of detachment before we all become connected fixtures in the Internet of Things. Soon we will succumb to its Borg-like reach, and become part of the collective via smart phones, iGlasses or, in the near future, body implants.

Everything Is an App Holder. The bottom line here is that as of Web 4 we need to begin to look at everything as an app holder. Things are now connected things, endowed with whatever capabilities of awareness, intelligence and connectivity we bring to them. My water bottle will tell me when my water has grown bacteria that can't be seen with the naked eye, or when my water supply is getting low, or when there are sales on bottled water wherever I shop. Traffic cameras that used to do nothing more than determine whether we were speeding will be able to tell whether we signaled when we changed lanes, or if we were driving erratically, as subjective a call as that might be. The cameras will relay video feeds of our movements to other street cameras, which will follow us as we progress down the highway. Intelligent software will synthesize the video feed to produce just the highlights. At some point a traffic infraction may result in your car effectively wearing an ankle bracelet, beaming information about your driving activities to the authorities, whose specialized software will determine whether or not you are meeting the conditions of your probation. In time we will come to accept this approach to law enforcement as normal, legally sound and even preferable.

In fact, the technology already exists that allows our cars to tell the police whether or not we are wearing our seatbelts. Heck, why bother telling the cops. They're busy. We'll just get a ticket in our email. Heck, forget email. Maybe we will just sign a user agreement provided by the Department of Motor Vehicles that allows the police department to automatically charge our credit cards. In exchange we may receive fewer points against our licenses, a practice not dissimilar to the Catholic Church's dispensation of indulgences during the Middle Ages. We are lucky to have escaped this so far. But when it comes, we will adapt to it. After all, we love it when surveillance catches the bad guys. The truly bad guys, that is. Not us. And we will particularly like the fact that this arrangement not only saves us money, but also saves us time.

Before we leave car talk, I should mention a recent news story about a Florida woman whose car used its 911 Assist feature to notify the police that it had been involved in a hit-and-run accident. When the car's airbags were deployed, 911 Assist automatically called her cell phone, which was pre-programmed to contact the police. When the police dispatcher contacted her at home, initially she denied her involvement. Then the dispatcher played her trump card when she asked her: "Well, why did your car call us saying that you'd been involved in an accident then?" Who are we going to believe, a human being with everything to lose, or a machine?

AI (Artificial Intelligence) Meets SHE (Sentient Human Experience). It's difficult to talk about the Semantic Web without also discussing artificial intelligence, also known as AI, which unfortunately I can't take the time to explore in depth. But it's important, so here's a brief introduction.

There are huge areas of research devoted to making machines that either simulate thinking, or actually do think, depending on your point of view. Much of the technology I have described so far uses some kind of AI. We see dramatic examples of AI in IBM's Big Blue, which defeated Kasparov at chess, and Watson, who won at Jeopardy and is now being repurposed to become a medical diagnosis expert.

We need to understand our part in building our AI-dominated future. As we use Google's search tools, we're not just serving our own needs; we're also training Google to become a better search engine. Google studies how we search and connect information within the Big Data deposits that we generate for it. This improves the AI used to process our requests, which in turn helps make future searches more effective. In the movie *Ex Machina,* AI engineer Nathan, who creates one of the world's first truly AI robots, describes the relationship we have with our search engines very well: "My competitors... thought that search engines were a map of what people were thinking, but actually they were a map of *how* people were thinking. Impulse, response, fluid, imperfect, patterned, chaotic." This is the world that our machines need us to help them understand, so that they can better understand and serve us.

Currently, an important question in the "AI meets education world" is this: Can student work be graded effectively by artificial intelligence? Great question. Low-level AI already can detect errors in punctuation and grammar and even style. Microsoft Word can already do this to a certain extent. But how about evaluating content, meaning and articulation? The AI industry is currently experimenting with these capabilities. AI-assisted assessment causes many academics to push the scholarly panic button. However, I must admit that having read upwards of a gazillion student essays in my day, I'm ready to have some kind of relationship with AI, though I am not exactly sure yet what I want it to be. We're back to the time issue. Wouldn't it make more sense to let machines do the grunt work in terms of grammar and spelling, and maybe even organization and basic thesis development, so that I can read for content, ideas and originality? Perhaps my personal robot will help me. Robotics is another "trend that bends" that unfortunately I don't have time to address. I'll just have to start giving longer presentations. There's the time issue again.

MOOCs, OACS and AI. Our need for machine-based approaches to assessment is driven by a number of developments, including the escalating cost of education, and the use of MOOCs (Massively Open Online Courses), which can enroll tens of thousands of students in a single course. The motivations behind MOOCs–access and inclusion, as well as branding and commercial enterprise–are basically well intentioned. The results are up for debate. I actually ran a MOOC, which I renamed an OAC (Open Access Course), about digital citizenship. (To see the course, go to jasonohler.com/digcit. Feel free to use anything you find.)

My conclusion about MOOCs? We need to redefine what it means to be educated before we will understand developments like MOOCs and OACs. In the traditional model of education, students were expected to complete the courses in which they were enrolled. However, now they go to the University of the World Wide Web to learn what they need to learn when they need to learn it. When students sign up for a MOOC, I don't think most are actually signing up to take a course in the traditional sense. Instead, they are registering to use an information service so they can take advantage of a body of knowledge that was organized by experts and informed by participants. They often take what they need from a MOOC and leave the rest. When they don't "finish the course," administrative systems see them as failures, even though students may have accomplished the goals they set for themselves. After all, they too are time-challenged. A clash of expectations occurs because "the system" takes a provider-centric approach to the course offering, while students approach the experience like customers. This clash may resolve itself as Webs 3 and 4 evolve. Intelligent assessment will be semantically distributed across systems; intelligent things will expand the kinds of activities that can be evaluated. In time, our activities may teach the Internet of Everything what it needs to know in order to evaluate our progress and skill level, summatively and formatively.

What are the connections and disconnections with the Semantic Web? I have talked about many of them. However, what we really need to keep our eye on is who defines the relationships that are established between the data points in Web 3, and the things in Web 4. Recall that everything by us contains our bias. This means that no technology is neutral because humans aren't neutral. Programmers and innovators will make cultural and value-based decisions, often unconsciously, whenever they develop new apps, create new gadgets and link networked elements in meaningful ways. Their decisions can inflect perspective about anything from social relationships to our attitude toward the environment.

Imagine conducting a semantic search for global warming that has a pro-development or a pro-environmental bias. That bias might be based on your previous searches, or Big Data demographic assumptions about you, or perspectives built into the search engine, intentionally or not, by its developers. The bias would surface in subtle ways, like excluding information we wouldn't expect to see, or putting important information we might find suspect in the last chapter of a semantic search report, where we are least likely to look. We wouldn't realize any of this was happening because the bias happens too far below the surface for us to see. TV channels have biases, so why not search engines? We could end up living in a kind of revisionist history without knowing it. Truth would become scarcer. Skewed perspectives, as well as outright lies, would become more difficult to detect. But we would love the time that semantic searching saves us.

The Semantic Web and Our Educational Future. The Semantic Web will usurp some of the tasks traditionally reserved for information consumers, like synthesizing and organizing search results, and providing new dimensions of inquiry by creating unexpected connections to knowledge that seemed outside the parameters of a search area. The result is that students will need to spend more time considering the accuracy of the information they consume, as well as the perspectives it portrays. Students will need to focus not only on connecting information and constructing knowledge, but also on deconstructing "finished search products" in order to understand their subtext. Understanding the nature of information itself will become a focus of inquiry.

Web 3 will open up opportunities to package and administer our own educations. Imagine a world in which courses are described semantically in all university catalogs, allowing us to draw upon multiple institutions to meet degree requirements. The smarter institutions will get into the business of evaluating and brokering educational experiences of many kinds from many sources. The world of alternate forms of educational certification, such as micro-credentials and badges, could flourish in such an environment.

How does the Semantic Web help our information-overwhelmed hero? She realizes it is going to make our overabundance of information and things far more connected and intelligent. It's going to make navigating the oceans of data that surround us a much smoother ride. And oh, the time it will save. However, she still wants to talk to whoever is in charge. She would like a way to be able to understand how data points and things have been connected, perhaps by having a search map that explains why certain searches produced certain results. She would like search engines to identify the nature of the relationships used to connect the data she receives so that she can understand the bias implicit in the search results. But for now she's cautiously okay with where the Semantic Web is headed. Onward over the narrative arc she goes.

Trend Four: The (xTreme) BYOD WearWare Movement

The next leg of the journey compels our hero to look very closely at her own life, and to take stock of all of the gadgetry that she has unconsciously incorporated into her daily routine. She lives a BYOD life, as we all do, in that she "brings her own devices" with her wherever she goes. She has to in order to maintain a continuous connection between RL and IR.

All My Stuff. A pile forms in her mind of all the iStuff she can't imagine living without, like her Wi-Fi-enabled iWatch and her FitBit fitness bracelet. Of course, the center of her BYOD universe is her smart phone, which is awash in apps she continually turns to without realizing she's doing so. She uses a number of social media every day to stay in touch with extended family members who are spread across the globe, and who will worry if a birthday passes without receiving one of her famous Happy Birthday singing eGrams. On her subway ride to work this morning she used an app to translate a business negotiation into proper Spanish; she used another to find potential hiking partners among the strangers who were sharing her subway car. All this happened before 8 AM. She wears her electronic enhancements like a suit of designer armor. When she considers trying to live without them, the thought makes her feel powerless...and naked.

Yet she knows that people used to get along just fine without all of this stuff. She has fond memories of listening to her grandmother talk about growing up happy during difficult times even though she possessed little more than her imagination and very few of life's basic amenities. She remembers her grandmother regaling her with tales of living without a TV or a telephone, and about gathering around the family radio to listen to some of the first broadcasts coming from some of the very first radio stations that ever filled the ether with music, news and DJ chatter. Her family's first radio was so heavy that two men were needed to lift it out of the horse drawn cart.

Yet, her grandmother did own a pocket watch that she carried with her at all times. It was her lifeline to a synchronized society, as well as to memories of her doting parents who gave it her as a high school graduation gift. We have always lived in a BYOD culture that reflects our times. Our distant ancestors carried flint and knives. Our hero's grandmother carried a pocket watch. Our hero carries the accoutrements of electronic accessibility and amplification that are considered normal in her day. Our BYOD culture will only intensify as our culture of innovation evolves.

BYOD Comes to K-12. This is particularly true in education, where BYOD refers to a movement that reverses decades of K-12 educational technology policy. Until recently, schools have assumed it was their job to provide technology for students. Now schools are beginning to expect students to bring their own technology to campus, the way my generation was expected to bring pencil and spiral notebooks to class each day. To understand BYOD's origins, let me provide a bit of history.

During the 1990s my fellow educational technology enthusiasts and I convinced school districts to buy desktop computers to "prepare students for the future." That first wave of computers looked like small army tanks with hulking, fuzzy CRT screens. Keyboards sounded like jackhammers and storage capacity was anemic. However, those early machines held so much promise for education that districts decided to purchase them using 10-year bonds. Unfortunately, the machines were obsolete five years later. In my defense, I warned school boards that this might happen, but was told that five-year bonds didn't yield enough return to attract the investment community. To make matters worse, not long after the first round of computers passed into obsolescence, I had to tell districts, "Sorry about that, but now you have to get laptops," which was followed a few years later with, "And iPads." Some districts simply started hollering, "Uncle! We give up! Students can bring their own stuff, and we will get out of the hardware business!" The worlds of business and higher education were already headed in that direction. Following their lead seemed like the only feasible course of action to take.

BYOD may have begun for financial reasons, but the inspiration that pushed it forward was the desire to personalize our electronic workspace to reflect our unique approaches to problem solving and productivity. If we were to look at all of our computers and devices, we would see that each of us has set up our workspaces very differently. You may have found a really cool piece of software I have never heard of. You most certainly have organized your desktop in a particular way that is unique to you. No two people's bookmarks are the same. Most importantly, we have set up our workspaces so that they can travel with us seamlessly, wherever we go, in ways that reflect our particular approach to living a digital lifestyle. Our children just want to be like us in this regard. Mass customization is the philosophical basis for BYOD, and the prime mover that disrupted a conformist culture that emerged in the post-modern era. In practical terms, this means that everyone comes to work or school with his own device that uses personalized apps running in a customized workspace. IT folks are in the throes of adjusting to this foundational change. When everyone used the same software installation running on the same computer platform life was predictable, even fixable. Not anymore.

On the user end, we are adjusting to becoming our own tech support, with the help of YouTube, chat rooms and our kids. Ultimately, we will put up with the tech issues of BYOD because we like the flexibility that it offers. We particularly like the lifestyle that BYOD facilitates by making it possible to manage our participation in all of the communities in which we are involved. The net result is that using our devices saves time…or simply allows us to do more, and thus overloads life, depending on your perspective.

Future xTreme BYOD. Where are we headed? I found a shirt online that offered a $20 option to become a WI-FI hotspot, allowing me to connect to the Internet through my clothes. It has been quite handy during our journey. Our hero confesses she may buy a hoodie she saw recently that would allow her to interact on Facebook through the use of body movements. She is also interested in an emotion vest she saw advertised that connects her to the eBooks she reads, so that she can feel what book characters feel. I must admit that the God Helmet looks tempting. Then there's the kissing bot. Let's not go there. All of these may seem extreme today. But tomorrow they will be invisible.

I have no idea how commercially successful any of these devices have been. But I do know that The Quantified Self (QS) movement is dedicated to helping its many thousands of members use specialized BYOD feedback devices to track and analyze health and wellness related data in order to modify their behaviors to improve their quality of life. They can collect data on a number of daily activities, including caloric intake (eating) and output (exercise); blood pressure and blood sugar; and sleep and air quality. Industry analysts predict that the fitness tracker market will be worth more than $50 billion by 2018, up from less than a billion in 2014, an increase of over 5000%.

The QS movement is a just a warm-up act for companies like dangerousthings.com, which sell biological enhancement hardware that turn us into "meta humans" by digitally and mechanically augmenting our eyesight, hearing and other capabilities. We can also buy tiny, implantable RFID (Radio Frequency Identification) chips that can connect our bodies wirelessly to our second, immersive reality. RFID is basically the same technology that is already used to track packages and pets, and activate security and recognition systems. Imagine passing your hand over an ATM to get cash; or walking within ten feet of your car in order to unlock the driver side door; or collecting information about yourself that would allow you to objectively assess your lifestyle to help you improve your diet and exercise habits. In a few short years, our world of BYOD has embraced wearware and "implantware." Indeed, the world of BYOD, which conjures up images of people running around with phones and laptops, is already beginning to look "floppy disk" quaint.

Companies who stand to gain from our boost in productivity may offer us incentives to "chip ourselves." Governmental agencies may promise to process our retirement payments more quickly if we agree to chip implantation. In many regards, RFID simply offers more advanced, invisible ways to perform a number of functions we already perform with our smart phones. Adopting RFID may actually end up being a very small step to take. It is important to remember that we don't need to be physically near something, like a credit card reader or a car, in order to activate a system. We just need to be near a WI-FI connection, which allows us to be virtually present anywhere, regardless of where we are in RL. RFID implantation will bring us one big step closer to ubiquity.

The future may be uncertain but our BYOD technological trajectory is clear. We will hack ourselves to "improve" ourselves, not only due to a sense of curiosity and artistry, but also due to our fear of not keeping up with our competitors, all of whom will have enhanced themselves in some way. In retrospect, companies like dangerousthings.com will be seen as the first affordable step toward Kurzweil's "singularity," a theory that projects that humans and technology will merge so seamlessly that they will become indistinguishable. At that point there will be no way for us to turn off our technology, any more than we can currently turn off a natural, biological limb.

By the way, we should expect new kinds of gatherings that

I call "hacking parties," where people share access to each other's sensory information through their bio-enhanced bodies. Imagine truly seeing the world through someone else's eyes and you get the idea. Bear in mind that anything that can be hacked can be hijacked. We already tap into cell phone calls and computer email; extending those capabilities to bionic eyes or RFID implants is conceptually and technologically easy to do. Anyone who can tap into our data streams can know not only where we are and what we are doing, but also what we are seeing and hearing. One day they will know what we are thinking and feeling. Who will use this information? As the narrator says in *Dark Net: Upgrade*, "Every bit of information about you is worth something to someone."

Perhaps most disrupting about xTreme BYOD is that much of it will be, in the words of technology guru Shelly Palmer, inconspicuous innovation. It will blend into our wardrobes and our bodies so invisibly that it will be undetectable during normal encounters. Will it become commonplace to scan one another before beginning a conversation, using another BYOD technology developed to detect the presence of inconspicuous technology? I assume so. We just can't be too careful these days.

While I am on the topic of how we can protect ourselves in a surveillance society, allow me to offer some advice. Suppose you are at dinner with someone who leans forward and whispers, "So, what do you really think of your boss?" I suggest you hesitate before responding. Perhaps you are being recorded or even broadcast through his glasses or contact lenses or the GoPro woven into his shirt fabric. Actually, it might be best to prevaricate. Lie, in other words. The optical recognition technology that makes much of AR possible, and which will most certainly become a standard part of our xTreme BYOD wardrobes, will become less obvious with each iteration. Eventually it will become so inconspicuous that we won't even know it's there. Some taverns have outlawed wearable recording technology in order to create a less inhibiting space for customers. The Motion Picture Association of America and the National Association of Theatre Owners prohibit recording by moviegoers and "...maintain a zero-tolerance policy toward using any recording device while movies are being shown." This works for the original Google Glass, which was quite obvious and a bit goofy looking. But how about future iterations of iGlasses, which may actually be contact lenses, or built into our clothes? In these circumstances such policies become unenforceable.

We're back to the math hat. Talk about xTreme BYOD! Are you going to buy it for your kids? You definitely are if all the other kids have math hats. What kind of parent would you be if you deprived your own child of the technology she needed to succeed? To make this decision easier for you, you will receive the math hat for free. It will be redesigned by Apple's Jonathan Ivey and look very cool. However, there is a catch: The math hat is going to stream the data that passes through it to Google and Nielsen, who may in turn sell it to math curriculum developers, all of whom promise to make sure your children's data remains anonymous. You may be surprised to find that you actually want developers to track your kids' academic activities so they can build customized learning modules just for them. You may be quite anxious to pay the $49.95 per month they require for such a service. So, now do you want a math hat?

BYOD and Market Research. There is no doubt that the future of consumer and education marketing research will use mobile, wearable BYOD. That's because current research methodology suffers from the Heisenberg effect: The process of observing something actually changes whatever you are observing. Researchers bring test subjects (they are no longer consumers) into a lab, wire them up, and then tell them to act naturally as they are shown pictures of smart phones, soft drinks and political brands. Reality? Gone. What do we expect?

Those seeking the truth in these kinds of situations need to get as close to the anthropological reality as possible. That is, they need to observe people in the process of being their unfiltered selves. Researchers want the "Candid Camera" reality. Our new, invisible video recording technology will make this possible, but with a twist. Instead of researchers recording subjects, customers will be the videographers, recording the world as they see it from their point of view. In this scenario, everything is recorded as they go about their business, and relayed wirelessly to the research office. Researchers parse the visual data and present it in terms like: "Eyes lingered on the Sumatra blend; picked it up, smelled it, put it back. Picked up the French Roast, smelled it, checked the price, put it back. Opened up the Columbia Supreme; smelled it several times. Didn't check the price. Put it in his grocery basket." Data like this is the holy grail for product developers because it represents not what we say we want, or how we respond to stimuli in fabricated research environments. Instead, it depicts how we actually behave. We have moved into a secording society, in which we can secretly record anything. I call this particular expression of secording "GoPro" Anthropology. The process of collecting the data further embeds all of us in a surveillance society, in which we never really know who is recording whom, and who will see the data. Do we really want to know all of this about ourselves? Perhaps we don't. But *they* do.

Is the future of learning research the same as the future of consumer research? We certainly will have the tech to make it so. Imagine students wearing "record everything" gear, going about their school day, showing where they succeed and where they stumble; where they linger and where they move ahead quickly; where they enjoy the experience and where they don't. Software will synthesize the highlights of the experience and produce a customized "learner facilitation report." Imagine a video readout like: "Student struggled with the quadratic equation for several minutes, fidgeting, tapping his pencil, and then clicked on the video option. After watching the movie, student moved quickly to the solution." Customized learning approaches would flow naturally from a synthesis like this. The use of these approaches could also change our current obsession with standardized testing. Instead of taking tests, students would just go about their business. Their activities would be deconstructed and analyzed for progress. They might never have to use a #2 pencil - or its digital equivalent - again. The doing would become the test.

I have already addressed a number of the connections and disconnections of xTreme BYOD. Now let's talk about how it can change education. To do so, I want to return to a question I asked in an earlier presentation: Do we want our students to live two lives or one? xTreme BYOD will compel us to address this question in very real ways. Currently, many students live two lives, a digital life outside school, and a non-digital life at school. However, those two lives will have to merge when invisible, smart, BYOD technology permeates our culture. At issue is how proactive we want to be about this development. In the future we will be judged by how well we helped our students blend their two lives into one inspired, safe, responsible approach to being human. But in order to help them, we must find ways to have them turn their devices on while at school. The flip side is that we also need to create a culture in which we also want to turn our devices off. As we charge into the BYOD world, let's create a balanced environment by branding BYOD "on/off." That is, let's find times to turn our machines on, and times to shut them down. Let's engage our students in conversations that don't require media. The art of direct conversation is an important pedagogy and a dying art. We need to keep it alive.

How does xTreme BYOD help our data overwhelmed hero? By providing her a highly personalized way to navigate Big

Data. She can do so on her own terms, using her own gear, which she chose and customized, which conforms to the kinds of sensory experiences and levels of involvement that she wants. All the other caveats about the unintended consequences of technology apply. However, for now she has decided that if she is going keep her head above water in an ocean of data, then she wants to use a floatie she has chosen, rather than one that someone else has given her. She continues her journey. But she is getting a bit tired.

Trend Five: Transmedia Storytelling

Our hero is already wondering how she is going to explain everything she has learned on her journey to others. She knows that a report or a stock PowerPoint presentation would never capture her experience. She has to tell a story. These days that probably means telling a "transmedia story."

What Is Transmedia? Given I'm addressing the nature of story in another presentation, here I will focus on the nature of transmedia. The term "transmedia" literally means "across media." However, in the world of modern media it is typically used to mean "across media channels and platforms." Transmedia describes a world in which media developers use every kind of medium and media channel available through the panoply of modern media expression to construct media that entertains, educates, inspires and promotes.

In their discussions of transmedia, media scholars often focus on the TV show *Heroes*. How many people used to watch it regularly but don't want to admit it in public? I see, all of you. How many are giddy with excitement about its return as *Heroes Reborn*? Same group. The show's creator, Tim Kring, said his strategy for developing and distributing content was to use every media channel available to him: television, social media, games, whatever was there. He called his approach, "using the whole buffalo." He involved RL, too. He would introduce a character for just a week, and then produce a traditional book that fans could purchase that was based on that character. He created a comic book to accompany each weekly TV episode. In addition, fans could purchase a sword like the one used in the show that displayed a paragraph that added to the show's narrative. The goal was to immerse fans in the show in every way possible.

Most importantly, *Heroes* involved fans deeply through social media, allowing them to make character suggestions, add pictures to the *Heroes* website, and become involved in a myriad of ways with the show's content. With *Heroes*, transmedia wasn't an add-on. Instead, it was part of the plan. Transmedia is standard operating procedure for media and entertainment developers now. That wasn't the case when the show started in 2006.

Transmedia guru, Henry Jenkins, put the mantra of transmedia very succinctly: "If it doesn't spread, it's dead." Let me get kinesthetic. Imagine I am wielding a butter knife the size of a ski and I am spreading a central story cannon across all the media in play: across Twitter, a TV show, a website, fan-based YouTube videos, games, you name it. Transmedia developers paint with a big brush on a very large canvas, which forms the background for much of our media expression these days. All media interact and cross-pollinate, creating an umbrella of experience. Some transmedia efforts are more organic than others, allowing fans to actually direct the story, add characters, and so on. But many commercial transmedia ventures control their story cannons tightly in order to advance the central story in very deliberate ways. As I mentioned earlier, we are ultimately headed for a transmersive media environment in which a synthesis of multi-media, transmedia and immersion is the norm.

In summary, transmedia storytelling spreads a central story cannon across many media channels and services. The channels are multimedia, social and personal, and accommodate whatever "now media" emerges in the mediascape. It is ubiquitous and blends RL and IR to form a story umbrella that covers us wherever we go. Transmedia depends on user engagement and an active fan base in order to thrive and evolve. And it is propelled by a compelling, engaging story that transports and resonates with the audience.

Every company or organization worth its salt has a transmedia storytelling strategy. However, we don't see transmedia employed much in education. Some questions before us are, "How could we use and coordinate all of the media channels typically used for entertainment, commerce and social organizations for the purposes of teaching and learning? How could we encourage 9th grade students to become "fans" of mathematics?" One of the greatest disconnects for our students between their lives at school and outside school revolves around these questions. The different media environments that students occupy are forcing them to lead two distinct lives.

Another important question is simply, "What does it mean to be literate?" It means being able to write "techxt" (pronounced "text"). I addressed this in depth in another presentation, but let me reiterate here that our baseline literacy has expanded to include the media collage presentation we see whenever we log on to the Web; we have no choice but to write whatever "techxt" our media compel us to write. Our greatest challenge as educational planners is figuring how to adapt more quickly to changes that expand our literacy landscape. We are already one revolution behind: While we were wondering how to assimilate the media collage into education, the baseline literacy expanded again to embrace transmedia. Now what? Literacy will keep expanding to include all the emerging media and communication channels that come along. How do we respond to this, and plan for the unforeseeable? The future is just getting started, and we have very little idea about what is coming next. Planning models need to be developed that expect the unexpected.

The issue of expanding literacy to include new media is hovering just outside education's door. Transmedia will break the door down. The transmersive media collage will absorb everything that developers throw at us. It has to. Our transmedia culture will demand that we adopt Art as the 4th R as new media becomes a generalized language with international, intercultural implications. Our transmedia culture will also demand that we cultivate "creatical thinking," which merges creative thinking and critical thinking into one integrated problem identification and solving process. Creatical thinking represents the "artistic viewpoint" that each of us needs to develop, regardless of what we do in our personal and professional lives. The current notion that critical and creative thinking compete with each other is crazy. We will need creatical skills to address all the challenges and opportunities that life presents us in our transmedia universe, personally, professionally and socially.

That covers some of the challenges of transmedia. Probably the most important connection it offers is access to our inner storyteller. Stories allow us to own our experiences. Life happens and we tell stories about it, whether that means explaining a math concept as shown in the earlier presentation about animating a rolling ball, or telling a story about a personal journey of exploration and redemption. We tell stories to synthesize events and insights in order to produce meaningful action. We must tell our stories if we are to stay emotionally healthy, intellectually engaged, and if we want to have a prayer of understanding and humanizing our current technological trajectory.

At the End of the Journey

Where do the five trends leave our hero at the end of her

journey? She finally feels somewhat fulfilled in her quest. Even though she's swimming in Big Data, immersion allows her to make meaningful connections among the data points in her world; the Semantic Web helps her manage and make sense of it through intelligent searching and connections; BYOD allows her to wade into the ocean of data on her own terms; and transmedia storytelling allows her to respond to her quest by allowing her to personalize her experiences and make sense of what otherwise might be chaos. The technological world that created her time-challenged lifestyle has also produced innovations to help her manage her time. She has traversed the narrative arc, overcome many challenges and transformed her understanding of the world. She has become more comfortable creating a personalized pathway through an overabundance of opportunity that would otherwise overwhelm her sensibilities.

She also realizes that one of the most effective ways to limit all of the information and technological opportunity in her life is to use a personal passion filter that allows her to focus on what she truly cares about. Her journey has enabled her to do that. Now she can begin turning the disruptive abundance in her life into something personal, manageable and meaningful.

However, she is still vigilant. She is engaged, but reflective. She wants tools that allow her to understand those who control the media, build the web connections, make the AI inferences, and bend the trends. She realizes that if she values truth and perspective, she will need to understand how those in charge of the technology see and program the world.

Forgive me for not addressing many tech trends including gaming, robotics, nanotechnology, 3D printing, and particularly singularity, Ray Kurzweil's term for the merging of humans and machines. Time simply didn't allow. But let me close with this.

We're back to the math hat. Let's say it has been redesigned and is now stylish or maybe even invisible. Let's say you can have it for free, with no strings attached. It won't be plugged into the Cloud, and won't beam your thoughts to anyone. Not Google, not Nielsen, not the government. The math hat is yours to keep and use as you wish. Now do you want one?

Whatever you decide, and whatever you do, please, go tell your story.

Thank you.

I D E A 4

THE ART OF THE STORY

Telling Your Story, Owning Your Narrative

Let's Begin with a Story

There are plenty of materials on the market devoted to the importance of using story in business, branding, organizational management, healing, education and personal transformation. But there are very few materials that actually explain how to construct an effective story. This presentation explores this topic in depth. So, without further delay, let me tell you a story. Afterwards we will discuss what made the story work, and then examine the three levels of story structure that permeate the narrative world: the story arc, the story core, and the mechanics of story motion.

Once upon a time there was a young man named William Tell. No, not that William Tell. A newer, more networked William Tell. He is the hero of my novel, *Then What?,* about finding a path with a heart in a world that is unnaturally overwhelmed by the unrelenting influx of iStuff. The novel begins with William assuming the helm of one of the world's largest financial sector computer networks at the mere, mid-adolescent age of sixteen. It was a time in his life when managing the information infrastructure of thirty-somethings just so they could afford their yacht payments felt like a huge distraction from the far more important goal of extricating himself from the existential angst posed by acne and advancing puberty. The fluke of events that propelled him to his position of preeminence are too detailed to describe here. However, it would be accurate to say that they consisted of the kinds of tawdry tabloid titillations that we'll never get used to but we just can't get enough of. Once the scandal dust had settled, and the tainted had fled, there stood William, the only one left in the IT department who had enough know-how to keep the vast network humming.

In this vignette from the book, it is five years later. We find William Tell on stage in the corporate auditorium during the company's annual Family Picnic Day. It's the same gig every year. The spouses, children, aunts and uncles of the company employees come to the corporate campus to drink stale cola knock offs, eat hamburgers on mushy white buns and watch whatever dog and pony show the corporation has created to entertain its guests.

This year William Tell has fashioned quite a spectacle. He spent the last ten months crafting the company's brand new, mega media, interactive, immersively hyper-linked, socially mediated, artificially intelligent website, and the family members were going to be the first to see it. He had reserved the great unveiling just for them.

However, as he stood on stage behind an oak lectern pecking away on his keyboard, a big problem was unraveling behind him. Although he could see the new website just fine on his laptop, all he could see on the two-story auditorium display that filled the back of the stage was a huge buzzing nothing. In his profession it was known as "the blue screen of death."

As audience members waited for William's new creation to appear, they became more fidgety by the moment, raising the din in the dimly lit auditorium to intolerable decibels. After all, they weren't executive types who brought a sense of corporate decorum to these kinds of events. No, no. They were kids hopped up on soda pop laced with high fructose corn syrup, screeching as they played first-person shooter games on their smart phones. They were socialites who hadn't seen each other since the last cocktail party, who were anxious to check in on who got what in the latest divorce settlements, and whether their kids had outscored each other on the SATs. As they trash talked their way through William's public mortification, they wondered whether they should cash in their stock options now, before it was too late.

William frantically pressed control this and control that. He reset every software app and reconnected every cord.

Nothing worked. Despite his best efforts to remain calm, he was perspiring so profusely that the sweat was rolling down between his body and his clothes, collecting in his shoes, making them slosh whenever he moved. He looked out into the audience and saw a row of adolescent boys with their baseball caps turned sideways who were chanting, "Loser, loser." He heard a woman in the front row say, "Well, Madge, let's go get ourselves a drink. No wonder Harold didn't get a bonus this year with bozos like this driving the bus."

As he listened to the audience grow hecklier and hecklier, he knew he had to act. He walked up to the microphone, cleared his throat and was on the verge of admitting his failure when a little girl, perhaps twelve years old, sporting pig tails and wearing thick-rimmed coke-bottle glasses, ran up to the edge of the stage and whispered, "Pssst! Pssst! Mr. Tell! If you hit Escape F12 three times, you'll reroute the video signal through the second com port and it'll come up just fine. Just another Windows bug. Yeah, you probably downloaded the patch from last night to fix the other bugs from the patch before that. Well, snap! That patch had bugs in it too and the patch this morning fixes the patch from last night. So you can go get the patch or for now just hit Escape F12 three times. Works like a charm."

William, just twenty-one years old, wondered, "How does somebody this young know all this stuff?"

But mostly he was focused on the indignity of the situation. Here he was, Chief Network Officer of one of the largest financial sector computer networks in the world, unable to load a webpage in front of an audience of parents and kids, and up walks a little girl who offers him tech support. There was absolutely no way he was going to take her advice. Self-respect simply wouldn't allow it. He looked down at her from his perch behind the lectern and muttered, "I'm a little busy right now."

"It's that old triple-encrypted BIOS," she sing-songed. "It'll get you every time. Do you need the patch? You can download

179

it or just hit Escape F12 three times."

"Yes," he interrupted her. "I heard you." He kept clacking away on his keyboard and checking his connections, burying himself deeply in the conviction that there was no way a little girl was going to tell him how to debug this moment in public.

"Hey, Mr. Tell, I might have the patch on my smart phone. Want me to zap it to you? 'Got Blue Tooth?'"

William watched an entire row of people near the back of the auditorium get up and shuffle toward the exit. All he could make out in their cacophony of cackles was an elderly woman saying, "I feel sorry for the boy. I hope he can keep his job. I've got a grandson in third grade who might be able to help. Should I call him?"

Suddenly he noticed a Barbie doll peeking out from within the folds of the little girl's cotton jumper. He swore it winked at him. It was the kind of off-kilter moment that made him wonder if he was really dreaming. He began to pray he was. The little girl noticed him staring and laughed. "I carry it around so people think I'm just another normal little girl. I turned her eyes into augmented reality cameras with 5-megabit connections. By the way, I hacked into your wireless system here. Piece of cake. I can show you how to plug that leak if you want. Anyway, back to your projector. Escape F12 three times. It'll work, honest. Why won't you just try it!?"

William looked down at the little girl, out at the crowd that was near mutiny, and back down at her. Somewhere in his subconscious he was wondering, why won't I just try it? What's my problem? With the sweat filling his shoes and the psychic tectonic plates grinding away in his soul, finally, in one fluid motion he hit Escape F12 three times and the web page triumphantly filled the auditorium screen! The audience erupted in applause. The adolescent boys with their hats turned sideways hooped and stomped their feet. The little girl hollered, "Atta boy, Mr. Tell! I knew you could do it!" William lifted her on stage and thanked her profusely. Barbie broadcast the moment on YouTube, where it was sure to go viral. And from then on, whenever he needed help with his computer, William Tell asked the computer club at the local elementary school to give him a hand.

The end.

Inside vs. Outside Stories

I tell you this story with all of its lack of subtlety so that we can deconstruct it and I can make a few points about how stories work.

To do this, let's back up and suppose that the problem had been that the cord between the computer and the projector hadn't been properly connected. William Tell plugged it in, and everything worked just fine. Would we have a story? No, because we wouldn't have the rising and falling action and the tension-resolution that a good story needs. Having a problem with the cord might kick-start the story if the cord had been broken, and the president of the corporation was rushing from the airport following a turbulent overseas flight just to see William present the new website, and there was only one other cord in the city, and William managed to get it just in the nick of time as the president took his seat in the front row. But just reconnecting a cord is too ordinary, and stories aren't told about ordinary events. Even the movie *Ordinary People* was about events that were extraordinary to the people who lived them.

What if William had willingly accepted the girl's advice, pressed Escape F12 three times enthusiastically, and solved his problem? Would we have a story? No, because we would be missing the absolute crux of what makes a good story work: transformation.

Let's explore transformation in depth because it is key to what makes narrative work. The story is off to a good start. It has a compelling problem, which a story needs in order to generate forward momentum. William desperately needs to solve the problem, and the pressure to do so is mounting. But the story doesn't really take off until the little girl walks up to the stage and challenges his authority. Of course, she doesn't look at it that way, but William certainly does. Most importantly, her actions give the story an "inside problem." This sets the stage for William's transformation.

Effective stories have both outside problems and inside problems. William's outside problem is to fix his computer. His inside problem is to overcome his resistance to accepting the girl's advice. Outside problems advance the events of the story, but not necessarily the depth or resonant quality of the story. Stories that truly engage us have inside problems that take us into matters of the heart and conscience, and involve us in the intricacies of interpersonal relationships. A hero's inside problems build a bridge between storytellers and listeners. As we listen, our sense of expectation is running full throttle as we wonder what the hero will do and feel next. In effective narrative, resolving inside issues enables story characters to overcome outside challenges. In this case, William's emotional transformation allowed him to resolve the technical issues with his computer.

Most importantly, the presence of an inside problem allowed us to gain access to William's psyche. This enabled us to root for him. We rode the moments of the story

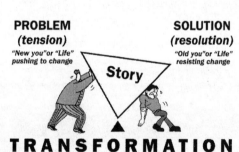

with him, waiting for him to transform because we wanted him to become a better version of himself. On a deeper layer, we imagined ourselves capable of the changes we wanted William to have the fortitude to embrace. We not only waited with him, we wait *as him*; his changes would become our changes. When he pressed Escape F12 three times, we cheered. When the little girl told William "Atta boy!" we were right there with her, and were as proud of him as she was. By extension, we were also proud of ourselves. Immersion in the transformation of the protagonist provides the kind of engagement that any advertiser, novelist, promoter, TV programmer, YouTuber or campfire storyteller hopes we experience. Done well, it is an exhilarating adventure for the audience that resonates long after the story is over.

Three Levels of Story Structure:

The Story Arc, the Story Core, and Story Motion

Implicit in my discussion above are the three levels of story structure: the story arc, the story core and story motion. The arc describes the broad sweep of the story; the core provides the overall dynamics within it, and story motion provides the details of narrative movement. Although all three are often developed in tandem, I am going to address each separately to help facilitate discussion about the role each plays in creating effective narrative. This mirrors the approach I typically use in storytelling workshops. I help storytellers focus on "drawing their story arc" first, before articulating the story core and the story details that materialize within it.

Story Level 1: The Story Arc

The arc is purposely broad so it can accommodate the dynamics and details of the story. At its most basic level, we should be able to describe a story arc in a sentence or two. Conventional Hollywood wisdom says that even a major motion picture should be able to be summarized in overarching terms, like: *Luke Skywalker resists becoming a Jedi Knight; eventually he realizes his responsibility to develop his gift so he can harness the power of The Force and save the galaxy.* A story arc is the elevator pitch we make to movie executives who need to know that our story idea is complete, and adequately embraces a story core (discussed in the next section). A story arc is also the ad concept, curriculum goal or media project summary we will want to clearly establish before beginning a project.

It is most instructive to understand the arc simply as a hill. I want each of you to draw an imaginary hill in the air in front of you, like that. Careful not to hurt anyone, including yourself if you have rotator cuff issues. You look beautiful out there. It looks like each of you is driving a car with a huge steering wheel. That is the basic story arc, and it stretches from the very beginning of a story to its last moment. Now, let me quickly add that the narrative arc is never as symmetrical or smooth as a perfectly shaped hill. Story arcs are filled with

BASIC STORY ARC

TRANSFORMATION

| BEGIN | GROWTH | END |
| Problem, question | Learning, experience | Solution, response |

peaks and valleys, as well as subtlety and subplots. Arcs typically ascend more slowly in the beginning, descend more quickly at the end, and rise and fall several times during the course of the story. For more anatomically correct versions of the arc, I refer you to my book *Digital Storytelling in the Classroom*, which shows a number of story maps, diagrams and arcs that I have collected over the years. However, the hill is the overall story shape that defines a narrative event.

Let's head inside the "arc hill" a bit to consider some of it mechanics. The hero starts at the bottom of the hill where things are relatively flat and calm, and where life is in balance. We don't think of the main character as a hero yet because nothing has happened to cause us to view her that way. Then something transpires that jumpstarts the story, often referred to in narrative parlance as "an inciting incident." Perhaps there has been a car accident, a storm, a house foreclosure, a divorce, an abduction or a physical threat; perhaps someone has won the lottery, been reunited with long lost family members or fallen in love. Whatever the inciting incident happens to be, it shakes the protagonist from her status quo, throws life out of balance and forces her up the hill where she will battle her way toward resolution. The trek up the hill is goal driven. If she is physically threatened, the goal is survival. If she is emotionally threatened, then it is to remain psychologically and emotionally whole. If her children have been threatened, then it is to make them safe. The goal defines her motivation. Her motivation allows us to see cause and effect in her actions, which allows us to connect her inside and outside challenges.

As she journeys up the hill, she encounters a series of challenges. She also meets guides and mentors, as well as antagonists and naysayers, who help and thwart her forward movement. Her experiences cause her to develop skills, perceptions and inner resources that sculpt her character. In the process, she learns and grows, and ultimately slays her internal and external dragons because her journey has given her the wisdom and strength to do so. She makes it back down the other side of the hill where life regains its balance. However, she is a new person. She has been transformed by her experiences and will never be the same. She has become "version 2.0" of herself.

While most story hills have a similar shape and flow, they can draw upon an unlimited variety of story materials. A hill can built on Luke Skywalker's refusal to accept his Jedi powers, or William Tell's inability to listen to a little girl who is trying to help him. Regardless of the nature of the hill, the act of scaling a story arc provides the outside challenges that frame the inside transformation–our hero may climb a mountain in order to mature and develop courage; or chase the bad guys in order to work out unresolved issues about her own failings; or pursue a love interest to bring to life long dormant parts of herself. She journeys up the arc knowing that everything that goes up must come down. After the story is over she settles into the new person she has become. Until the next hill.

The Digital Storytelling Arc and the Magic of Healing. Our discussion of the arc provides an ideal segue for talking about one of my favorite storytelling adventures: conducting digital storytelling workshops with mental health clients. I have worked in the digital storytelling arena with thousands of clients, from 8 to 80 years old, from elementary school to PhD students, for the purposes of education, personal transformation, organizational management and commerce. But my favorite adventures have been working with mental health clients. They are deeply involved in slaying dragons and developing inner, transformative resources to overcome the often overwhelming challenges in their lives. Their hills are quite formidable. Their stories are always tragic and inspiring.

Before continuing, let me define digital storytelling simply as using your own laptop, touch pad, smart phone–whatever you have–to mix images, music, video and your recorded voice into a coherent narrative. Digital stories often have a documentary look and feel as we listen to narrators walk us through events that they illustrate using images and video. The stories I help clients create are very accessible on a practical level–they rarely require a budget, can adapt to whatever production values time allows, and focus on story, rather than the gear and glitz of media production. Fortunately, creating a digital story doesn't require much technical expertise. The last workshop our team conducted used iMovie on iPads. We trained a group of participants who were not very tech savvy in less than twenty minutes.

I was introduced to the possibility of using digital storytelling for mental health healing many years ago by the director of a mental health clinic. She had seen my work helping students create media and speculated that therapists and media teachers could work together to help her mental health clients create digital stories that were empowering and therapeutic. From the outset, the results were remarkable and rather unexpected. Her clients, many of whom had suffered extreme abuse and had developed a number of negative behaviors as a result, disclosed deeply and eagerly about highly personal experiences. They did so in ways that were risky, revealing and healing, as well as helpful to the therapists who were trying to aid in their recovery. Nearly all clients were asked to post their work publicly on YouTube so that the rest of the world could benefit from their insight. Clients had been living inside their own stories and needed to create a new story for themselves that helped them shed their old selves and see life through a new lens. Creating a digital story was their chance to do so, and to build a pathway to their own transformation. As a result of making their stories, clients often reported feeling better, clearer, lighter and liberated. Each of them reported a desire to create more stories. To this day, conducting these workshops is the most gratifying work I do.

It is important to note that living within our stories is a reality we all share, regardless of our life experiences. Each one of us has crafted a narrative about who we are and who we aren't, as well as who we can and can't become. Often, our stories are based on the stories others tell about us. Their stories are often expressions of their hopes and limitations, not ours. The result is that our story arcs bind us in ways that we can't see. Recall my earlier discussion about McLuhan's figure-ground theory, "figure" being what we focus on and "ground" being the invisible environment that envelops us entirely and massages who we are in subtle, pervasive ways. Our story is our ground, as well as the story hill we assume we were destined to traverse. It is the emotional and psychological container in which we unconsciously live. For this reason, our stories define our possibilities. The most effective way to change our story is to make it "figure" by telling it aloud, at least to ourselves but preferably to others. In the process of telling it we bring it to the surface where we can see it, understand it and change it. Think of rewriting your story arc as an exercise in creatively reprogramming your possibilities. We all live within our story arcs. That will never change. However, we can always change the nature of our story and who we choose to become.

Before turning to the details of fleshing out the arc at levels 2 and 3, I want to emphasize three aspects of the digital storytelling process that made it so effective with the mental health clients. Incidentally, these aspects also apply to any group with whom I have worked. However, they are especially powerful with this particular clientele.

First, we required clients to begin their projects by creating a story map (essentially, a very detailed story arc) that spanned a particular event or period of time, and which described their overall transformational journey in basic terms. We'll look at the specifics of story mapping tools later on. However, suffice it to say for now that the story mapping process basically involves sketching "a hill" on a piece of paper, or talking through the specifics of the story arc with a counselor. This "arc map" then became the crucible within which levels 2 and 3 (the story core and story movement details) played out. Recall the *Star Wars* story arc described earlier, which captured an entire movie in a few sentences. A personal story arc works in the same way. With our clientele a story arc might be as simple as "Once upon a time, I was abused by a partner. But I sought help, which gave me the strength to leave the relationship. I emerged a new person, stronger than before and committed to never subjecting myself to abuse again."

Second, clients were required to integrate two parts of themselves in order to become digital storytellers: their reflective selves and their practical selves. Their reflective selves had to dig deep inside their experiences and revisit unbelievable pain in order to get close to it, understand it and give voice to it. That is, they had to confront difficult "inside problems" that, in many ways, had come to define them. Their practical selves had to rise above their pain and focus on a number of practical activities, like collecting images, making voice recordings and finding appropriate music. Solving these kinds of "outside problems" kept clients focused on completing their projects. The net result is that the emotional storyteller and the rational producer had to work together to create a final product. They kept each other on task.

Third, using digital storytelling workshops transformed the structure of therapy from one-on-one counseling to participation in a cooperative art studio. Implicit in this structure is the belief that clients are artists and storytellers with important narrative to create and share. In fact, sharing is key. Every workshop holds a group showing at the end. It is a moment of triumph for participants, many of whom have incorporated an expectation of failure into their assumptions about the future. Group showings are always compelling, engaging events, and often form the basis of relationships that evolve after the workshop.

Story Level 2: The Story Core- Problem, Transformation, Solution

The arc forms the story's super-structure; the story core provides its backbone.

A story core consists of three basic components: problem-transformation-resolution. We saw the core drive the forward momentum of William's story. He had a problem on two levels. His outside problem was that his computer didn't work; his inside problem was that he couldn't accept the advice of a little girl who was trying to help him. He transformed by overcoming whatever personal issues prevented him from accepting her advice. These issues may have been sexism or ageism, perhaps compounded by practiced insecurity and unresolved childhood issues. Who knows? In a longer piece we may have explored these more deeply. However, the point is that his transformation is what allowed him to press Escape F12. Without his transformation, he would still be on stage stuck within his old persona, dealing with the aftermath of his failure.

Once you develop an eye for the story core you will see it everywhere–in ads, in books, in movies, in TV shows and in the more interesting stories that we tell each other. It is so pervasive because it resonates so effectively and universally.

Ads? Aren't they a bit short to contain all the detail I mentioned earlier about journeying up the hill? Perhaps. But fifteen seconds is plenty of time to portray an elevator pitch that embodies a clear story core. In fact, one way to look at ads is to see them as stories in highly concentrated form. There are a number of ads in which a customer is reluctant to try a product (the hero resists) but is convinced by a friend or salesperson (the guide) to develop a new understanding of the product's value (transformation) and change brands (to resolve his problem): someone's cleanser isn't working; on the advice of a friend he tries another, realizes it is better and changes brands. Problem-transformation-resolution. This is not a story you will tell your kids, but advertisers are hoping that using the highly resonant, universal story core will work its magic by commandeering our psyches on a deep level, making it more likely that we will remember the ad experience and buy their products. After all, awareness and attention precede acquisition; unconscious awareness is particularly powerful. Advertisers are betting that providing information in story form will be more effective than presenting it in list form, that is, than simply listing a product's attributes. People like stories. They don't much care for lists. Most importantly, people remember stories much more easily than they remember lists.

What does a story without a transformative core look like? As I explain to storytelling students, the opposite of a good story is a slide show of someone else's vacation. We've all been there. We're invited to a friend's for dinner and suddenly find ourselves immersed in a blow by blow retelling of his trip to Grandpa's cabin by the lake: Now we are in the canoe; there's the paddle we dropped in the water; oh no, look at the snake on the rock! And so on. The basic structure of the presentation is the list: this happened, then this happened, then that happened. Unless we were on the trip, we are simply listening to a series of irrelevant events that have no inherent story shape or transformative quality. We pray for the onset of a severe headache so we can excuse ourselves from the festivities.

Grade B action flicks also often lack transformative cores, using good versus evil as a central theme but providing little else to go along with it. Perhaps the hero transforms by becoming a bit more sensitive or falling in love in the process of killing the bad guys. However, transformation is a minor subplot, not a focus. The point is that stories without a transformative process don't provide a way for us to become emotionally involved with the characters and the narrative. We are left to ride the events. To the extent that riding the events entertains us (as the hero and antagonist slug it out, or a car chase keeps us riveted to our seats), then action films can work. But riding the events is all we get. There is very little that sticks with us after the story is over.

Resistance and Relatability. In the story told earlier, William resisted changing, a common trait among story heroes. A hero's resistance allows us to watch his growth unfold. It also gives rise to the tension that makes us lean forward in our chairs and fixate on his development, desperate to see how he will ultimately address the ego and angst that keep him from overcoming his challenges. We can relate to William's reluctance to change because we resist similar kinds of change ourselves due to pride, ignorance or any number of personal challenges.

It is William Tell's relatability that allows us to identify with him.

Let me emphasize two points about "relatability," given that it is key to a story's effectiveness. The first comes from media specialist, Kathy Craven: use the small story to tell the big story. The story I told is just one, brief incident in William Tell's life. Yet it is microcosmic, and tells a much bigger story that relates to his life and ours on a macro level. Telling the small story is a very practical approach to narrative. It limits the details and time period storytellers need to address, while allowing them to make big points. They can use a handful of specifics to paint a picture of universal meaning that everyone can relate to.

The second point is the following cardinal rule of storytelling: Audience members become deeply involved with narrative when the story they are listening to becomes their story. This level of relatability goes beyond simply being able to identify with a character. In visceral terms, we need to feel a character's pain. We need to enter his emotional ecosystem. Note that we do not need to have lived through the specifics of William's dilemma in order to identify with him. Our connection with him comes from the fact that we too have found ourselves under pressure in publicly embarrassing situations. It is the feeling that this situation generates, not the details that comprise it, that provides the connection between William's experiences and our own.

On a very practical level, the first step in establishing relatability is to take advantage of our natural tendency to 'willingly suspend our disbelief,' as the poet and literary theorist Coleridge described it. A cornerstone of the human condition is our natural desire to leave the mundane world behind in order to enter the realm of narrative fantasy. Effective suspension opens the door to "transportation," a psychological theory that claims that effective narratives transport us into story so deeply that we fuse with the characters, often experiencing a complete loss of self. Wherever the characters go, we go with them; wherever the story takes us, we become part of the narrative caravan. The phenomenon of transportation accounts for the disorienting feeling of re-entry that we experience when a movie ends or we put our book down and are suddenly thrust back into real life.

Story Level 3: Story Movement- Motion Inside the Story

We arrive at level three, story movement, through which much of the detail of story plays out. Here we will consider how the ebb and flow of events within stories maintains our sense of narrative engagement. To demonstrate how this happens, let's do an exercise in building a story. More specifically, in rebuilding a story. I'm going to tell a bad story so that we can convert it into a story that works by using the principles of effective story motion. In the end what we create may not be a great story, but it will be an effective story.

When I do this activity with young audiences, I always begin by asking them three questions. The first is, "Who would like to hear a story?" Everyone raises their hands. No surprise here. Who doesn't want to hear a story? Compare this response with the one you would get if you offered to read a report or recite a list.

Then I ask, "When I tell you this story, do you promise to be honest with me about whether or not you like it?" Everyone pledges to be honest. I ask younger audiences to pinky-swear, and they do so willingly. Lastly, I ask them, "Okay, and what are the parts of a story? I just want to make sure I have it right." Invariably, every audience chants the same narrative litany: beginning, middle and end. I hear it over and over. I understand. That's how we have been trained. Hang on to this misleading oversimplification. It will become important a little later.

Okay, so here we go. This story is called *Uncle Albert and the Sandwich Party*.

Once upon a time there was a young boy named Thad whose mother sent him to the bakery to get two large loaves of bread because Uncle Albert was coming over for sandwiches, and Uncle Albert always had such a voracious appetite. Thad put the silver coin his mother gave him in his pants pocket and made his way to the bakery, led by the sweet smells of breads and cakes that beckoned him. When he arrived at the store, he greeted the storekeeper, paid for two large loaves of Buttermilk Brie bread and skipped home.

Later that day, Uncle Albert arrived with a voracious appetite, and the three of them feasted on cucumber sandwiches, hogs feet and pickle sandwiches, peanut butter and peach cobbler sandwiches, and all kinds of delectables captured between two slices of bread. They all had a splendid time, regaling each other with stories and fun. They reminisced about family holidays, and birthday parties filled with balloons and banana cream pies. When late afternoon arrived, Uncle Albert announced regretfully that he had to go home. He had to feed his six cats, water his plants and put a log on the fire so his house would be warm for the evening. Uncle Albert heartily thanked them both, hugged his sister, shook hands with his nephew and headed out the door. Thad and his mother cleaned up the dishes, swept the floor and then played Scrabble until dinner, which consisted of leftover sandwiches galore. The end.

Beginning, middle and end. They are all there.

As the students listen to the story I can see in their eyes that they are waiting for something to happen. When I declare "the end" they look at each other as if to say, "Is he serious?"

At this point I turn to them and say, "Okay! Did you like the story?" I can hear them sweat. On the one hand they don't want to be impolite to a guest and, for younger audiences, to an adult. On the other hand, they had promised to be honest about whether or not they liked the story. The reality is they didn't like it, which speaks highly of their narrative discernment abilities. In plain speak, they know a bad story when they hear one. Eventually one brave student comes forward and says, "I thought that was really boring." Then an avalanche of objections ensues that basically say, "that was sooooo boring!"

I ask them to help me deconstruct and reconstruct the story in order to revitalize it and turn it into a story that isn't so boring. I begin by asking them, "What's the story missing?" I wait to hear the magic word: problem. Exactly. The story had no problem.

The word "problem" is an umbrella term that includes obstacle, challenge, goal, question or anything that makes us lean forward and wonder what's going to happen next. Because our story doesn't have a problem it has devolved into a list of related bullet point events that hang together but take us nowhere.

The audience and I walk back through the story. We follow Thad down to the store. He grabs the loaves of bread, puts them on the counter, reaches into his pocket and...oh no, the coin's gone! He's lost his money! What's he going to do now? Then we brainstorm solutions to that problem. With enough encouragement from me, the participants generate incredibly inventive ideas. They suggest our hero work at the bakery, panhandle, do some kind of street performance for tips, sell his shoes, ask the baker for mercy because aliens sucked him into their spacecraft and stole his money...you name it. The students could brainstorm forever if we had time.

I'm directing the activity, so I wait until I hear what I need. I always do: Someone suggests he should go back and look for the coin, and that becomes the idea that the students and I decide to use.

Then we retrace Thad's steps and...*there's the coin.* But darn! It's beneath one of those metal grates that you see on city sidewalks that allow you to look a few feet below street level. Our hero thrusts his arm through the grate to try to grab the coin. Ugh, he can't quite reach it! I ask students to pretend to try to grab something just out of reach, and to make straining noises as they do so. You try it. Reach down in front of you, and try to grab the coin. That's it. Oops. I heard someone hit his head on the seat in front of him. We're not going for that kind of realism here.

Thad's natural instinct is to try to lift the grate. He wraps his fingers around the cold, hard metal of the grate and tries to pull it up. Go ahead and try to do that where you are sitting. Feel that cold hard metal in your hands. Feel your muscles strain. Grunt as you lift. When telling stories, paint a picture with words and sounds that engage the senses. Appealing to audience members' senses helps them feel what the characters are feeling. It bonds storytellers with story listeners.

"Ugh!" he grunts as his strength gives out. Thad just can't quite lift the grate on his own. Now what's he going to do? Once again I ask the group to come up with ideas. Again, with my encouragement, I hear the most amazing ideas like Thad should get a helicopter with a winch, rent an elephant, get a robot with a giant magnet or see if he can pick up the coin using chewing gum stuck on the end of a stick. Eventually, we accept that he needs to get help to lift the grate.

I continue the narrative by telling participants that as our hero looks around him he sees only one person on the entire street: Mary. Uh oh. He doesn't get along with Mary. Last year he stole her lunch, she called him buffalo breath, and they haven't talked since. Actually, he just took her apple, but she loved apples. The experience left her not only hungry, but also deeply offended.

I introduce the situation with Mary so students have an opportunity to compare and contrast inside and outside problems. Until now our story has had only outside problems, like locating the lost money and figuring out how to pick up the grate. The story needed an inside problem to really pull us into the narrative. Thad's interpersonal issue with Mary, and his need to solve a problem on an emotional level, provides that inside problem.

Again, I invite students to brainstorm. Again, I hear very interesting ideas. Thad could beg Mary for help. He could offer to do her homework, plagiarism issues aside. He could apologize and hope for the best. If that didn't work, he could threaten to spread falsehoods about her on Facebook. Kids can be mean.

Eventually the class and I settle on the idea that Mary and Thad need to resolve their differences and get back on track with their friendship. After extensive negotiations, during which Thad apologized for his thoughtlessness and Mary graciously offered to forgive and forget, Mary and he managed to lift the grate together. Thad invited Mary to come home with him for lunch, and off they went to share sandwiches with his mom and Uncle Albert, who always had such a voracious appetite. Thad made sure Mary got an apple. No, two apples. The second paid for the accrued interest on the one he took from her last year. At the end of the activity I hope I have not only helped students understand how a story flows, but also have provided a brief lesson on problem solving, interpersonal communication skills and applied ethics.

Let's look at the interior of our story. No doubt many of you have heard narrative described in terms of "rising and falling action." Stated simply, stories never sit still. They move up and down. Story motion appeals to our natural attraction to movement. We won't stare at a tennis ball sitting still on a table for long, but we will watch a tennis match for hours. Our attraction to motion is tied to survival, and comes from the need of our "ancient human" to continually scan the horizon for signs of danger. Our fixation on movement keeps us pinned to the moment so that we can find out what happens next, as it happens. Most story motion comes in the form of movement and resistance to that movement, which provides the tension-resolution dynamic that stories need to be engaging.

Let's consider the movement in this story. Our poor hero. All Thad wanted to do was go to the store, get a few loaves of bread and go home. Yet, he was challenged every step of the way. He got to the store, but he'd lost the money! He found the money, but it had fallen through a grate and he couldn't reach it! There was someone who could help him, but she didn't like him! It's like life was out to get him! In stories, life often is. As he tried to move forward, life resisted his movement. As audience members, we rode the rising and falling action with him like we were surfing the waves of a roiling body of water. The medium of movement, more so than the message or the details of the plot, keeps us engaged. No motion, no involvement. However, motion combined with a great message and interesting details is one of the holy grails of narrative.

Once you understand rising and falling action, you will see it everywhere. I have worked with students as young as second grade who could very successfully "draw the mountains" of a cartoon. Roadrunner did this, Wile E. Coyote did that. You will see this dynamic whether you are watching cartoons, sitcoms, epic movies or documentaries; or whether you are reading novels, comic books or well-crafted investigative journalism. Some of my storytelling students have told me that thanks to my story training, the patterns of rising and falling action in movies have become so obvious that they dominate what they see. The result is that my students have difficulty "transporting into the narrative" and simply enjoying the show. I really didn't intend that to happen. Please, continue to enjoy movies.

Time for an activity break. Please draw rising and falling action in the air in front of you. Careful not to poke anyone. Use your finger and go like this: up and down, up and down, rising and falling action, like you are drawing mountains in the air. Now, in your mind, draw your day. You drove to work, but traffic was heavy. Someone called you on your cell phone, but your phone was in your pocket. You managed to get it out of your pocket, but had to process some guilt about driving and talking on your phone at the same time. The caller turned out to be your daughter, who called to say hi but also to tell you that she had forgotten her credit card and couldn't buy lunch. You called the school's receptionist to okay a purchase with your card, but were very reluctant to leave a voice message on their automated system that identified your credit card number. Finally, you got to work, but there were no parking spots left. You had to drive around the block a few times, but finally found a place to park. It was actually closer to your office than your normal parking place, but it cost twice what you were used to paying. You move forward, life resists. You resolve an issue, but another appears. Life rises and falls. These are small events, and perhaps not story worthy. But this is the kind of motion that moves stories along and allows us to ride the narrative. Choosing just the right events for your story is part of the artistry of plot building. But regardless of the events you decide to include, they must have motion.

Another perspective of rising and falling action comes from story theorist, Robert McKee. He says that a story moves towards its goal, and then away from its goal as it advances the overall plot. I describe it as narrative zigzag. Characters head toward a particular destination. Zig. As they do, life blocks them in many forms, from a collapsed bridge to a collapsed self-concept. Zag. Movement-resistance. Characters zigzag their way over the arc.

In her TED talk *The Secret Structure of Great Talks*, storytelling expert, Nancy Duarte, deconstructs speeches delivered by Steve Jobs and Martin Luther King to reveal a similar kind of rising and falling pattern in their narrative. In her model, their speeches move up and plateau as they emphasize and expand on certain points. Then their speeches move back down in order to make the next rising point more salient. Regardless of how you chart and describe story flow, the point is clear: Without movement and counter movement, narrative doesn't have the motion necessary to sustain our attention.

How about positive stories that basically move in just an up direction? They may be positive stories, but they are also flat, boring stories. Just to make this point very clear, let me provide an example of what happens when rising and falling action isn't present, even in an upbeat story. Suppose I created a documentary about a camping trip that went something like this. Day one. It was a great day. Everyone was getting along, everyone's socks were dry, there was trail mix for everybody and butterflies filled the sky. Day two. A great day again. The sun was out, there were even more butterflies and not a discouraging word could be heard from anyone. Day three. It was another great day...

At this point, you are reaching for the TV remote to change the channel because you are bored out of your mind. The issue here is that the story kept going towards its goal, towards its goal, towards its goal. All zig and no zag. Boredom causes us to disengage. So does mistrust. We inherently distrust a story like this for the same reasons that we inherently distrust promotional materials, or overly optimistic quarterly reports. They don't ring true as stories. We can't relate to them. They don't remind us of our story. They threaten to waste our time.

This story would have worked much better had it unfolded like this. Day one. The campers were having a great day, until the wind blew away their tent. Fortunately they found a cave nearby where they could sleep that night, but strange sounds coming from inside the cave made them fear that animals were already living there. They managed to get set up inside the cave, but realized they had lost all of their bottled water. There was a shallow creek inside the cave, but they didn't know whether the water was safe to drink. A conversation ensued about the water, which quickly became a heated argument about *why were they on that stupid camping trip anyway when they barely knew each other and weren't even really friends!* The health of the camping trip was clearly in peril. The estranged, mistrustful campers had to figure out how to get along if they were going to solve practical problems of survival and have any hope of enjoying themselves. And they hadn't even reached day two yet. From a narrative perspective, this situation brings together a very effective combination of inside and outside problems. In addition, the campers' situation is much more realistic and believable, as anyone who has been camping will tell you. If their days had been filled with nothing but sunshine and butterflies, then they might have a story to share with their friends. But the rest of us wouldn't want to hear it.

The bottom line is that time is precious and we could always be doing something else. Maintaining attention is everyone's goal, whether you are a storyteller, a spouse, a marketer or a friend. Every company's nightmare is user disengagement. In the digital age, disengagement happens quickly and often unconsciously with the click of a button or a tap on the screen. How do we engage an audience to give us a chance? By using a well-developed story that moves up and down, through the hills and vales of a journey.

Summarizing: A story is built on a broad arc that carries the narrative from one end of an experience to the other. The arc houses the dynamics of the story core

STORY ARC
Rising and falling action, combined

BEGIN   TRANSFORMATION   END

(problem-transformation-resolution) that drives meaningful

action and character development, which in turn allows audience members to make deep connections with the story. Permeating both the arc and the core are rising and falling action that carry the flow of the plot. The story arc diagram shows how all three story levels work together to form an integrated narrative. It is an example of a story map, a tool we will discuss later, that facilitates planning stories quickly and effectively.

I should note that this presentation focuses primarily on a more traditional, hero-based expression of story. There are many other less mainstream approaches to narrative, including music videos, absurdist drama and virtual world stories in which the lines between storyteller and story listener blur. Discussing these would be a fascinating and important digression to undertake. Unfortunately, we simply don't have time. If you are interested in this area I recommend reading the chapter I devoted to this topic in my book *Digital Storytelling in the Classroom*.

It's time for some more physical activity. Because you are the advanced group, we're going to multitask. Draw the arc with one hand. Let's see the big steering wheel. At the same time, draw the zigzag of rising and falling action with the other hand beneath the arc. Let's see how you do. The arc with one arm, rising and falling action with the other. Okay, that didn't go well, but you get the idea.

Four Foundational Story Concepts

Before I launch into some of the tools that I use to help people create stories, I want to address four foundational concepts concerning story and story making that should help you with your own work.

Foundational Concept 1: Lists vs. Stories

We are awash in different forms of narrative, from epic

sagas to hyperlinked transmedia to bullet points. Instagram, CreateSpace and Twitter embed us in the fabric of a universal broadcast space. The oracle YouTube entertains us with memes like Gangnam Style (over two billion hits), instructs us with do-it-yourself car maintenance advice, and fills us with the wisdom of Ted Talks. Augmented reality, bio-enhancement and all the new media and technology that our imaginations will bring forth will continue to broaden our storytelling horizons in ways we can't imagine.

One approach we can use to frame our continually evolving media narrative is to assume that it will always change. This approach focuses on the evolution of the technology. We can use this approach to build hierarchies and taxonomies of innovation that can help us understand the past in order to better predict the future.

Another approach to understanding our ever-expanding narrative universe assumes little has changed or ever will change. This is the world of Dertouzos' ancient human. Instead of focusing on the technology we focus on the nature of the narrative that the technology conveys. There are several ways to frame this approach, one of which is particularly helpful to us here: considering the world of narrative as a continuum that stretches from lists to stories. Media may come and go, but this continuum has remained rather consistent over the years. The primary difference between lists and stories is that stories integrate information much more easily than lists. This is a critical difference because human beings recall information more easily when it is integrated rather than presented in discrete pieces.

A colleague of mine in the branding business demonstrates the power of integrated information to his clients using the following simple exercise. He splits a group of clients into two subgroups. He presents ten words to one group in list form, and the same the words to the other group in sentence form. When he asks participants to recall the words, typically he finds that those who saw the list remember very few words, while those who saw the sentence can recite it in its entirety. The magic of the sentence is that it placed discrete, disconnected words in a connected context, which in turn made them more memorable. Without context, we experience chaos. Context also provides meaning, and without meaning, human beings are emotionally helpless. Stories succeed largely because part of the bedrock of the human condition is the fact that human beings will avoid chaos and seek meaning at all costs.

The following example very clearly demonstrates the utility of placing information within the context story on a larger scale. I was working with an organization that wasn't having much luck getting the public to engage with one of its PR campaigns. The organization was trying to educate the public about the fact that children who ate breakfast before coming to school did better academically than those who didn't. The children who showed up hungry were so poor that their families couldn't afford to feed them. The campaign was in support of a school breakfast program.

When I asked to see the campaign materials that the organization's PR team members had developed, they showed me colorful pie graphs and detailed statistics. I yawned. I told them that I knew I should care but I didn't. Not yet. I told them that their campaign was only going to work if they presented their details within the context of a story. Further, the best way to approach the story was to create a hero who had a problem, and who was transformed in ways that empowered him to solve his problem. Audience members would then engage with the story because they wanted to know how the hero was going to overcome the challenges he faced.

By the end of our afternoon together, the organization's campaign had changed radically. It had been recast as a story about Juan, who dreamed of becoming a doctor, but would never be able to attend medical school because he was too hungry to focus on his school work. Problem: Juan was hungry and couldn't focus. Solution: feed him breakfast. Transformation: breakfast changes him physically, emotionally and intellectually, allowing him to think and function at full capacity so that he can grow up to become a doctor. Then, after presenting the story, the campaign can show the charts and statistics that reveal how many people like Juan there are in our school systems. The audience's transformation is to realize the unfairness of Juan's situation and hopefully recognize a call to action. The most powerful stories are those in which not only the characters transform, but we also transform along with them. This kind of impact is one of the primary goals of effective storytelling: The characters change and we do, too.

The approach the PR team used was simply an extension of the principles at work in the "words in a list vs. words in a sentence" branding exercise explained earlier. By conveying statistical information using story as a vehicle, the team gave important but otherwise dry and disconnected facts real context and meaning. My synthesis of much of the neuro research I have read over the years boils down to this: We are built to favor information in context because of the meaning it provides. In other words, we are designed to favor stories as our primary information container. I don't know whether the group I worked with that afternoon ever used the new campaign about Juan that we had designed. But had they, and had I seen an ad like the one we designed, I would have leaned forward, listened and supported their campaign.

Converting lists to stories as a narrative approach is applicable in any field. In terms of education, recall my earlier description of fourth graders using animation software to create a rolling ball. At first, they didn't succeed: the ball skidded instead of rolled. Then they applied a more complete understanding of math to their calculations, and the ball rolled successfully. If they had used the "list form" approach to reporting their activities, then they simply would have shown the steps needed to make the ball roll successfully on the first try. However, the students introduced a problem into their piece, which required that they transform by learning more mathematics in order to get to their solution. As a result, we became much more engaged in their story than we might otherwise have been. The bottom line is that when students show not only what they learn but also how they learn, their work takes the form of narratives and stories, rather than lists and reports. This approach is not only a much more effective learning strategy, it is also much more interesting to us and to them. Most importantly, when students create narrative about their learning we more clearly see how they think, create, and learn. In turn, this allows us to be more effective in terms of how we become involved with their education.

Incidentally, the next time you want to engage an organization in strategic planning, think in terms of creating a movie that describes how you want the future to unfold. Imagine the movie begins today and concludes at the end of your planning cycle, probably one to three years from now. Imagine the hero of your movie is a student, client or member of the public you are trying to serve. You don't have to actually create the movie. That's a lot of work. But just thinking in terms of creating a story in movie form will help you focus on the arc you want your organization to traverse, the story core that needs to drive its transformation, and the rising and falling action you might need to anticipate. The fun part is thinking about who gets to play you when your movie goes Hollywood.

Foundational Concept 2: Stories Are Who We Are Psychologically, Emotionally, Culturally and Neurologically

Concept number two is that story has not only emotional and psychological appeal, but also an innate neurological basis. Neuroscientists like Drs. Paul Zak, Michael Gazzaniga and others have conducted fascinating research that looks at the chemistry and neurobiology of the brain as they relate to storytelling. Let's consider just Gazzaniga's work for a moment.

Gazzaniga studied epilepsy patients who had undergone surgery to disconnect the two hemispheres of their brains, a procedure used to stop the firestorm of neural activity that gave rise to their epileptic seizures. One of his research questions was, in so many words, "What does each half of the brain control?"

He discovered that each half handles specific responsibilities and doesn't fully know what the other half is doing. He also discovered that the left half of the brain has a particular function, which is to serve as the interpreter or the story-telling brain. It interprets events by placing them in a narrative context that isn't necessarily supported by the facts. That is, we tell stories about our stories. We live life normally, moving forward in real time, and our interpreter brain follows behind us, knitting together a story to place our activities in a narrative context. We could simply use lists to describe what happens to us, but on some very deep level we have made the decision not to. We need our actions to be connected. Only a narrative approach can do that. Again, it does seem that our need for story is at our very core. But this time not only the psychologists are telling us this is so; the neuroscientists are as well.

While the science behind our need for narrative may amaze us, we really shouldn't be surprised by the revelation that humans have a predisposition toward story. It's easy to imagine humans evolving to favor strong storytellers over weak storytellers. Presumably they could convey information more effectively, form bonds more readily and assume leadership positions more easily. It is not difficult to imagine that storytelling was a skill that wielded power and influence back in the day, just as it does now. It seems that story is part of Dertouzos' "ancient human."

Because we now understand that we have reasons to favor story that are neurological and biological as well as emotional and psychological, it seems reasonable to project that our need for story will be as prevalent in the future as it has been in the past. I've been in the technology world for over thirty years and have found that innovation comes and goes, becoming useless and quaint very quickly. But one thing that will never change is the need for a good story, a fact that recent developments in transmedia storytelling and immersive reality make only too clear. As I said earlier, the only thing that I know for certain about the technologies that await us in the future is that we will find ways to tell stories with them. This reality of the human condition will transcend whatever future innovation we might imagine.

Foundational Concept 3: Words and Media Work Together

As a storytelling teacher, I focus on helping storytellers develop their stories as written narrative *first*. Adding media comes afterward. This is a time-honored approach to media development that has always worked for me. However, the importance of the interplay of narrative, images, sound and other media cannot be overstated. In the words of educator Beth Stansky, "...pictures use a visual language to tell the story and the words use a verbal language to paint pictures. Often one language enhances the other."

In fact, for many years I have had to sell digital storytelling to schools as an activity focused on written literacy, when in fact it also involved visual literacy as well as several other forms of media expression. The problem was that visual literacy didn't sell very well in our "3 Rs" testing culture. I once had a heated discussion with an administrator who was committed to the belief that art and visual representation were just not as important in today's work world as having a facility with words and numeracy. I asked him where he obtained his information and he showed me a website that was replete with sound, images, video, design and navigation, as well as text and numbers. Gently, I tried to explain the contradiction in what he said and what he was showing me. It didn't go well.

The following anecdote provides a low-tech example of the importance and expressive possibilities of deliberately combining image and narrative. I was working with a client who was creating a short movie that began with her dog pouncing on her when she came home from work, a ritual that apparently happened every day. To depict this event, she showed a photograph of her dog sitting in the kitchen as we listened to her recorded voice explain how antsy her dog became after spending a long day cooped up alone. On the surface, this image seemed well aligned with her narrative. She was talking about her dog and we were looking at a picture of her dog. But I suggested that in order to bring her narrative to life she take another photograph that was shot from the perspective of her lying on the floor looking up at her dog as he jumped on her. With help from a friend, that evening she managed to snap a photo that perfectly captured her dog's enthusiasm. The photograph provided a much better articulation between image and narrative. And it was an action shot, which always engages viewers.

This is just one very specific example of combining narrative and image. But it is representative of a much larger world in which a number of media combine to form the language of the media collage. In our transmedia world, audio and visuals are just the beginning. Each form of "now media" will demand its own kind of literacy. Yet, we don't teach this or test for it. The reality is that either we learn how to read and write using these literacies, or risk being illiterate.

How we approach the use of story media depends on our goals, audience and message. A more "image centric" perspective says we should develop both words and images simultaneously, rather than writing the story first and adding images later. If the goal is to teach visual and written literacy so that students develop a sense of how they inform each other, then this approach can be very effective. Sometimes we can use images that are so strong that they compel narrative, or images that are so powerful that they don't even need written or spoken narrative. But for most of us in most situations, the "story first" approach, as described by the arc and articulated by a script, is where we start. It provides the foundation for all that follows and provides the greatest promise of producing articulate, professional media.

Foundational Concept 4: Story First, Media Second

I have been teaching some form of digital story telling ever since the Apple IIe was available. If you know what an Apple IIe is then I am going to assume you are members of AARP. I hope you received a senior discount on your conference admission. If you don't know what an Apple IIe is, consult an old person or Google, the great oracle. As I mentioned earlier, the IIe was a fabulous machine and to me was the first personal computer to be both lovable and useful. But enough reminiscing.

During my early days of digital storytelling I noticed something very interesting: As the technology became more powerful, in many cases my students' stories became weaker. It seemed that as students became more enamored of the gadgets and the glitz, they became less focused on what they wanted to say. The situation brought to mind Einstein's quote, "Confusion of goals and perfection of means seems, in my opinion, to characterize our age." This kind of technical distraction was happening with students of all ages, from eight to sixty-eight. It became urgent that I find ways to bring the story into digital storytelling.

My first step was to invite expert oral storyteller, Brett Dillingham, to work with my students. He told stories, explained performance standards and technique, and deconstructed how and why his stories worked as they did. Keep in mind that he was teaching my digital storytelling students how to tell traditional, oral stories. However, that didn't seem to matter. As a result of his training I saw an immediate improvement in the quality of my students' media-based stories. Convinced of the need to teach students storytelling principles as part of digital storytelling training, I translated what I learned from his training into the planning tools and methods that I address later on.

Although narrative structures are similar across media genres, story production details differ profoundly depending on the types of media that are involved and the extent to which they are used. The use of media is a double-edged sword. On the one hand, media editing programs act like assistive technology for the aesthetically challenged like me, who needs a tool like Photoshop in order to draw a recognizable stickman. On the other hand, what happens when you give a bad guitar player a bigger amplifier? If you don't have something to say then your media will just magnify that reality. I have seen beautifully produced pieces that have no story; the high production values they used actually made their narratives worse. I've also seen well written media stories created with very low production values that have moved me to tears. The bottom line here is this: The technology needs to support the story, not the other way around. Story first, media second.

The great American philosopher George Clooney summarized the importance of basing movies on solid stories during in an interview in which he was asked to respond to the question, "What makes a good movie?" In so many words what he said was this: "I really don't know. But here's what I can tell you. I can take a good story and a good script and turn it into a bad movie any day of the week. What I can never do is take a bad story and a bad script and turn it into a good movie, I don't care how much money you give me." These are wise words that translated into my world very well. The net result of my process of adapting traditional storytelling to digital storytelling was to create very simple planning tools that could help my storytellers stay focused on the story and not get lost in the glitz.

Typically, my students create some form of digital story that mixes voice-over narration with video and still images, producing media that resemble documentaries. This approach to production is fairly straightforward and folds fairly easily into the flow of a regular day, whether at work, home or school. I also do performance based, green screen storytelling, which involves storytellers recording their original storytelling performances in front of a green screen so they can show images behind them, much the way weather announcers use green screens to show the weather maps and other images that accompany their broadcasts. When working with students, a "green screen" is often just a wall that has been painted green using whatever paint was available from the local hardware store. There is no need to use anything fancier or more expensive than that.

In post-production storytellers slide original artwork behind their recorded performances using "chroma key replacement software," more commonly known as "green screen software," which is now a standard feature in most video editing programs. The final product is a video recording of storytellers performing original stories in front of their own artwork. Green screen storytelling involves a good deal of writing, re-writing, rehearsal, image development and other research, planning and production activities that we value in education and the work place. Green screen storytelling is labor intensive, but worth every minute of it. It is a compelling demonstration of the DAOW of literacy described in an earlier presentation.

A Word About Storyboards. I find that most audiences have some understanding of storyboards. Therefore I will be brief in my description.

Typically, a storyboard is a media planning document that looks somewhat like a PowerPoint presentation. On each slide appears an image that represents the action, images are accompanied by notes about a number of aspects of production like camera angles, music and sound effects. Clicking through the presentation steps you through the story, so you can make sure you like how it proceeds before you begin all of the expensive production work.

If you work in professional media you are expected to create storyboards for a very good reason: Large scale productions require large scale plans. However, most of us are working on a much smaller scale and neither need storyboards nor have the time required to create them. I have talked with a number of educators who won't get involved in media production with students because they are convinced they need to create involved, time-intensive storyboards. They don't, as the next section will explain. Another issue with storyboards that I have discovered over the years is that very few can "read them" well enough to determine whether the events they describe work together as a story. Being able to do so requires a kind of artistry of its own. The result is that storyboards often tend to do nothing more than make boring stories flow logically. For these reasons, I suggest you move away from storyboards and toward some of the tools that I am about to introduce. I think you will find them faster, more efficient and more accessible to you, your students and your clients.

Story Planning and Production in Four Steps: Map, Script, Table and Production

There are those rare people who, like Mozart (or so the romanticized version of him goes), can produce exceptional work without much planning. The reality is that most of us need to use a detailed planning process to create successful media projects of any scope and detail. "Plan your work and work your plan," friend and mentor Daniel Malick told me long ago. When we plan our stories they tend to be more professional and articulate than if we had created them on the fly. And they tend to be better stories.

In this part of the presentation I am going to get very practical about the tools and methods I use to teach storytelling, as well as to use storytelling as a communication strategy with clients. Note that the tools that I'm going to feature can be used to plan any kind of story using any kind of media, from traditional oral stories to movies. In addition, they can be used in any setting, from business to education to mental health. It is important to note that these tools specifically offer a media planning layer, should you decide to translate your story into a media format. You can use this layer, or ignore it, as your needs dictate.

I use a four-step planning process: creating a story map, writing a script, making a story table, and producing a digital story. We will begin with story maps.

Step 1. The Story Map – Visualizing the Story Structure

The primary purpose of the map is to combine the three levels of story structure into a single visual guide. As the story arc diagram shows, the "arc" provides the overall meta-structure of the story. It provides a crucible for the three elements of the story core, as well as a means to frame the details of plot and the zigzag of story movement. Practically speaking, you can create a story map on a piece of paper (the value of this low-tech approach is explained just ahead) and either include the labels "problem, transformation and resolution" on your map, or at least keep them firmly in mind as you are developing your map. You can annotate the map with plot activity using words, phrases and even small images–whatever works for you. The goal is to provide the overall flow of story events in your own terms without having to use full sentences or detailed descriptions. After all, one of the benefits of this planning approach is that it is much faster than using storyboards, and more easily fits into your busy schedule.

While using story maps is helpful for anyone, it is particularly helpful for younger students who often "hit the sentence and paragraph wall" rather quickly after being asked to write a story. I encourage students to use whatever form of shorthand makes sense to them to minimize any frustration they might encounter with the writing process. In curriculum-speak, the story map is an effective pre-write. A story map is also a great "back of the napkin" tool for anyone who wants to capture the essence of a story idea.

The "arc map" shown earlier is very popular. However, there are many other story maps, a number of which I describe in my book, *Digital Storytelling in the Classroom*. One very popular map is the "visual portrait of the story" (VPS) by Brett Dillingham, which uses the outline of a circus tent to map a story. Imagine giving the story arc "cat ears" and you get the idea. I have adapted the VPS for digital storytelling planning, as well as for general story development purposes. One of my storytelling students in Fielding's Media Psychology PhD program, who works for a major branding company, has incorporated it into his practice in order to help clients clarify their mission and goals.

Sometimes students create original maps. For example, one student used the outline of his house. His map depicted him walking through his childhood home, which allowed him to explain the challenges he had experienced with his family, before making peace with the past and exiting through the back door. Brilliant. Another student used the outline of a human body (imagine a gingerbread figure) to map her story. Her narrative began at the tip of one hand, then split and simultaneously moved through the head and the heart as the story unfolded. Her story map captured the conflict she experienced about a major life decision that involved her rational and emotional selves wanting to go in different directions. In the process she explained what she learned and how she resolved her conflict before both paths reunited and exited the other hand. Also brilliant.

A story map is basically what you need in order to pitch an idea to an executive producer, because you need a hundred million dollars to hire Bruce Willis to play the lead in your movie. Or to pitch an idea to your boss or a group of colleagues in order to gather support for a project. The story map allows project managers and narrative developers to convey their ideas in terms of their essential components very easily, and to ensure that team members are all on the same story page. Teachers who use story maps tell me that they can look at their students' maps and tell very quickly whether or not they have the potential of becoming solid stories. The clarity of the story map allows them to debrief with students and offer feedback that is simple and helpful.

Part of the process I use with students and clients involves peer pitching, a process I adapted from Nikos Theodosakis' book, *The Director in the Classroom*. I ask writers to work in groups of three or four to pitch their stories to each other based on their story maps. They critique each other's stories based on this question: Are the problem, transformation, resolution and events both clear and interesting? Some of my favorite moments as a teacher have been eavesdropping on those conversations and hearing comments like, "Hey, Bobby, how about you have the giraffe instead of the elephant fly the helicopter?" This is exactly what I want to see and hear: students working collaboratively, using their maps to improve each other's stories.

Earlier I mentioned that I don't recommend clients use

computers to create story maps. I find that the story can get lost once the brain starts jumping between free flowing ideas and the details of manipulating software. Instead, I ask students to create maps using no more than pencil and paper. This planning approach "front-end loads" the digital storytelling experience with a story focus before production begins. Incidentally, my online students send me pictures of their hand drawn maps via their smart phones. That approach works just fine.

Step 2. The Story Script- Writing the Narrative You Will Speak

The next step in the planning process is creating and writing the script for your story based on the ideas you have captured with your story map. Because digital storytelling typically uses voice-over narration rather than video-recorded actors, a digital storytelling script takes the form of a word processing document that you will read and audio record, rather than a typical movie script that identifies actors and their lines. About three minutes are required for most people to read a one-page script that is written using double spacing and a 16 point font size, and which is well spoken, paced and nuanced. In my opinion, this length suits most digital stories and media forms. I prefer the sculpting model to the painting model, which requires storytellers to chip away excess material in order to reduce stories to their essence.

There are many practical reasons to think about the amount of time required to listen to a story, particularly the decreasing attention span of, as far as I can tell, just about everybody in the world. In a Twitter universe populated by headlines, substance needs to be delivered quickly. The exception to this is movies; if they are any less than 90 minutes long we feel cheated. However, stories in most other forms need to be brief. If you are a teacher, story length becomes particularly important because you're going to need enough time to evaluate each student's work. That is why I suggest that students create stories that are no more than 3 minutes in recorded length. This length restriction changes, of course, if students are in a media class creating formal media for major projects.

Step 3. The Story Table- Aligning Story with Media

After writing your script, the next step in the four-part story development process is creating the story table, my replacement for the storyboard. Actually, the story map and story table combine to create a simpler, but more comprehensive and useful replacement for the storyboard.

To visualize a story table, imagine a simple word processing table that consists of two columns. In the left-hand column is your script. In the right-hand column are production notes. "The game" is to create a new row in the table whenever the image on the screen changes, to which you can add notes about whatever images, music, or sounds will accompany your narrative. In addition, you can add images in the row, so you can see your images and narrative side-by-side. When you have finished your story table you have produced a script, a media list, and production notes all in one simple word

Written Text for voice-over	Images, Media
Once there was a student who wanted to tell a digital story, but didn't know what to talk about. She thought - what would be interesting to her?... to her audience?	*image of myself gazing off & wondering*
At dinner she asked her parents for some help. They told her about her grandparents and a few embarrassing stories about when she was a baby... but still nothing was quite what she was looking for...	*image of family seated at table... myself, with embarrassed look on face*
Then she had an idea to visit a psychic...	*psychic & myself huddled around crystal ball... spooky music in background*

processing document. This is an incredibly efficient approach to story planning, and much faster than building storyboards. It is important to note that what I am presenting here are guidelines, not rules, and you should adapt them to your particular situation and your particular process. For example, if you are pressed for time, then skip the Word Table and simply print out your script and add production notes in the margins. Adjust as you need to.

An important concept to keep in mind when developing a story table is "media alignment." The goal and challenge when creating any media-based story is to lead with the story, and use the media to support and align with the narrative. In the best media pieces, narrative and media work seamlessly to support each other. Yet, all too often I see media projects in which production overwhelms the story. This is particularly unfortunate for those who are using media to give voice to a personal perspective. Therefore, my focus is in helping storytellers articulate their story first, and then aligning media to support it.

Step 4. Story Production- From Plans to Product

With your story table completed, production begins. Notice that until this point the production process has not required story developers to use the computer for anything other than word processing and perhaps some web searching. Most importantly, up to this point, we have not needed to use any media development software. As I said earlier, once media production begins the story can take a back seat. Using a story planning process that limits reliance on media production software until production actually begins helps to prevent this from happening.

With a few notable exceptions, like working in the mental health field, I usually don't provide hardware and software. Workshop participants bring whatever media editing software they already use on whatever machines they already use so they can keep working on their projects after the workshop ends. Besides, there are so many ways to create media these days that trying to standardize on a particular platform seems pointless. Rarely, I will need to jumpstart someone's media editing skills by introducing them to one of the many free media software packages that are available through the Web. However, the challenge of software familiarity has abated over the years. I find that most attendees come to workshops with enough knowledge of a media app to be able to go to work. To help participants take advantage of each other's talents, I begin workshops by polling them about their skills and then posting a "talent list" that shows who is good at Photoshop, iMovie and so on.

Recording Your Script. Typically, production begins with recording your script; images, sound and video are added afterwards. I have seen participants try to reverse the process by placing images in a media editor first and then narrating around them. But this approach rarely works. Speak your narrative first.

Because the narrative forms the foundation of your media piece, it needs to be narrated well. Unfortunately, this is not a natural tendency on the part of many first-time narrators. I've heard many storytellers read their scripts as though they were in fifth grade droning their way through an essay titled, "A Good Time I Had with My Parents this Summer." It doesn't matter whether you are reading a script for a digital story, or you're standing on stage presenting to an audience, or you're in a boardroom trying to make a point; your voice needs to be paced. It needs to be nuanced. It needs to be inflected. These qualities bring motion to your speech, which keeps us engaged. Our voice is the most powerful tool in our multi-media toolbox. We should help students develop their voices so they can tell their stories with clarity and humanity, and so they can develop the oral presentation skills they will need in their personal and professional lives.

Production Values. This term refers to the overall technical quality of media production. It covers a vast area that I simply don't have time to properly address. However, here are a few comments that should help you frame your further exploration of this important aspect of media expression.

Earlier I mentioned media grammar, a topic I explore in depth in my digital storytelling book. It is the term I use to refer to many of the production value considerations that we encounter as media teachers and producers. I have seen a number of grammatical transgressions over the years, a few of which are worth mentioning as a kind of "fair warning." At the top of the "please don't do" list is playing music that contains lyrics while the audience is trying to listen to spoken narrative. The result is cacophony. Why aren't the storytellers confused when they listen to drafts of their own work? Because they already know the story and have no problem distinguishing between the two voices. In contrast, audience members are hearing the story for the first time and literally have to "ear squint" to pierce through the confusion. If you must use music with singing then stop narrating while you do so.

Also at the top of the banned list is the inappropriate use of music, like playing something upbeat while talking about a serious subject, or simply using music that does not align well with the narrative. Mediaists should ask themselves, "What music would best support the story?" and then find music that meets that objective. This is not difficult to do in our era of plentiful, copyright free music. However, what they usually do is work backwards from what they have on their phones to what they use in their stories. Basically, their feeling seems to be that the music they carry with them is too handy not to use. This approach often results in the mixing of music and narrative that don't align very well, producing a "reverse engineered" look and feel. In a sentence, the goal in professional media is to use music that sets a narrative tone and mood that supports the story.

Another item near the top of the banned list is the gratuitous use of effects, filters and transitions, like fisheyes and barn doors that slap us in the face and completely take us out of the narrative when we see them. When I ask students why they use effects like these, they often say, "I don't know, but aren't they cool?"

If students have issues with media grammar then I give them TV watching assignments, much to the dismay of language arts teachers. Note that "TV" refers to any form of professionally produced media, and can be watched on any of the screens that populate our lives. The goal of my media watching assignments is for students to observe how professional mediaists address issues like using music, transitions and other elements of media production. As a result of their critical viewing exercise, students inevitably see what I hoped they would see: singing and speaking rarely occur at the same time, transitions are so subtle as to be unnoticeable, and effects are appropriate to the action. That is, nothing they saw or heard jolted them out of the narrative. My goal is for students to create media that is as professional as time, equipment and budget allow. I want them to create professional media for the same reason I want them to write articulate essays and conduct well-researched science projects; because this is what professionals do.

The Media Maturity Line. From an emotional development perspective, my job is to help students of all ages cross the media maturity line. That is, they need to approach the media they create not only as something they want to say but also as something others will need to understand. They need to make sure that their approach to content and their use of technique helps rather than detracts from that goal. In terms of content, telling a story that does not connect outside one's experience fails in this regard. In terms of production values, recall my earlier comments about the clash of music and spoken narrative, and the inappropriate use of music and transitions. Media makers need to be able to ask themselves, "Would someone who is not living inside my head understand this?"

The consideration of the audience perspective in the planning and production process can be quite a leap in maturity for some to make.

Evaluating Media. What follows are four pieces of advice about assessing media projects that I have found very helpful over the years. First, don't give an A for anything that moves on the screen. I can't tell you how often I watch the following scenario unfold: Teachers, awestruck by a student's video, get that oh-my-god look in their eyes, automatically give the student an A, and slowly back away from the computer. Teachers do this partly out of fear, partly out of respect. Their response is very well intentioned. They think to themselves, "I don't know how to do that technically; therefore, I need to give them an A." Rubbish.

Teachers need to approach students' use of gratuitous technique as teachable moments in media literacy, as well as media production. Teachers don't need to be the most capable computer geeks in the room any more than coaches need to be able to outplay their best players. They simply need to be discriminating, articulate consumers of media, and have the fortitude to tell their students, "That doesn't work. The music is too loud and I can't hear what you're saying." Or, "You're talking about a dog but I'm looking at a picture of a cat." Initially, students rarely appreciate my candor when I am honest with them about their work. They are used to adults who praise their efforts without really saying why, or engaging with them about the quality of their stories or production in a meaningful way. However, along with honest critiques I also provide helpful suggestions about how to create more articulate media. By the end of their projects, typically students are very appreciative of my perspective. But while they're in the midst of production, they sometimes they have their doubts. I have learned to be patient with their process.

Incidentally, I watch similar scenarios unfold in the

business world, where I have seen far too many presentations that were big on razzamatazz and short on story. This is an utterly misguided approach that ignores thousands of years of evidence about the importance of story to the human psyche. Spectacle may grab our attention, but it can't sustain it.

A word of caution. While demanding professionalism from our students and those in our charge, we also need to be prepared to be challenged by new forms of expression that will continually emerge in the "now media" era. There are many ways to tell and interact with stories these days. Our technologies and story platforms will continually evolve and expand our notion of narrative involvement and expression. However, if our goal is to tell a clear story, rather than to develop an abstract poem or concept piece, then everything I have said in this presentation about how to create articulate media still applies. It applies whether story developers are creating a game, a digital story, a transmersive environment, or some new form of narrative we can't imagine yet. I predict that I could come back in one thousand years and find that we would still honor a good story much the way we do now. In order to prove this though, I need some of your students or employees to invent a time machine.

My second piece of advice for evaluating media comes in the form of an observation. I find that it's impossible for me to effectively evaluate both the story and the production values of a media piece at the same time. Therefore, I have to evaluate each media project twice. First, I watch for the story. As I do, I make notes about the articulation of the story core as the narrative traverses the arc and rides the "what's going to happen next" zigzag. Then I watch the same media piece a second time immediately thereafter to assess production values. Because I already know the story, and am not waiting to see what will happen next, I can step back from the story and focus on how well it was constructed. I can pay close attention to issues of media grammar, like the use of music, solid narrative, transitions, etc. The bottom line is that you may need to leave more time for the evaluation process than you might think.

My third piece of advice is to analyze and evaluate everything students produce in the process of creating media, not just the final project that we see on the screen. This includes evaluating their research and writing, as well as their images and speaking–that is, all aspects of the DAOW of literacy. If handled professionally, a single media project provides an opportunity for students to develop a very rich, multi-layered portfolio that spans traditional and new media literacies.

My fourth piece of advice has to do with "finding stories by asking questions." Sometimes workshop participants tell me, "I don't have a story" and become what I call "story stuck." Sometimes I will ask them to create a story about not having a story. These stories have been some of the best I have ever heard. But the reality is that they have many, many stories to tell–we all do. Their challenge is finding them and choosing one to develop. I often assist the "story stuck" by helping them identify a question to kickstart their narrative journeys. The process of identifying the question often leads to important stories they want to tell.

Even banal questions engage us, despite our best efforts to resist them. "Have you ever wondered why you have so many different cleansers under your sink?" an Amway representative might ask. No, I haven't ever wondered about that. But now I do, even though I would really rather not spend my time thinking about it. Or, "People all over the world are tired of waking up tired after a bad night's sleep. And do you know what they do?" a mattress company might ask. Despite the fact that you're sleeping just fine there is some part of you that now wants to know, gosh, what do they do? You can't help it. This is the power of a question at work. A question is the zig that begs a zag. The content is less relevant than the story's movement. It is the zigzag motion of the question-response structure that engages us. All questions wake up the brain. But imagine beginning a story with a truly important question, like, "Who am I?" Or, "How can I build the best robot on the planet that is smart and kind?" Or, "What should real education for the 21st century look like?" Or, "Why do clouds behave the way they do?" Or, "What is the math of a rolling ball?" Or, "Who do I want to be when I grow up?" There is no shortage of important questions to ask.

Bottom line: If you are stuck for a story idea, then start asking questions.

The Eight Levels of Transformation

To me, story events exist to support the transformation of the hero, not the other way around. We are interested not only in what heroes do, but also in what they realize. Both are necessary and important, but we are moved primarily by how story characters change and grow. The difference between action and realization is the difference between food and nutrition. The events are the food, the transformation provides the nutrients.

What does transformation actually look like? I have identified eight levels of transformation that I have distilled from the many stories that have flowed through my life for so many years. The eight levels are not mutually exclusive. They often overlap, travel together and work in tandem to provide different layers to stories and story characters.

The First Level Is Physical or Kinesthetic Transformation. At this level, characters develop a strength or dexterity. Popeye eats spinach and grows muscles. Baby (Jennifer Gray) in *Dirty Dancing* learns how to dance. William Tell learns a few new keystrokes. Luke Skywalker (Mark Hamill) becomes more adept at wielding his light saber. Frequently, transformations at this level are accompanied by higher order transformations.

Luke Skywalker didn't just learn better moves with his light saber; he also grew in many other ways, too. But keep in mind there are always bad movies that don't rise much above this level.

The Second Level Is Inner Strength Transformtion. At this level, characters overcome fears and develop courage. Recall the movie *Gladiator*, in which Lucilla (Connie Nielsen) and Proximo (Oliver Reed) helped Maximus (Russell Crowe) in his effort to restore The Republic. Initially, neither had the courage to help Maximus. Eventually they summoned up the fortitude to do so, at great risk to themselves. As they developed their courage, we felt it with them. We rallied behind them. We imagined ourselves being as courageous as they were.

The Third Level Is Emotional Transformation. At this level, characters mature and think beyond their own needs. Han Solo (Harrison Ford) returns to fight the good fight in *Star Wars*. In *Road Warrior*, Mad Max (Mel Gibson) overcomes his selfishness and returns to the community to aid in its survival. In other words, they mature emotionally and they grow up.

The Fourth Level Is Moral Transformation. At this level characters develop a conscience. We see echoes of this in prior levels of transformation, like inner strength and emotional growth. But growth at this level becomes very powerful when characters make a deliberate moral statement–like Schindler (Liam Neeson) developing his list, or Norma Rae (Sally Field) rallying her fellow workers to organize against inhumane working conditions. One day, in the textile factory in which she and her co-workers slaved away in miserable conditions for miserable pay, Norma Rae started a revolution. She stood up and a union was born. And we stood up with her, convinced of the moral righteousness of her cause.

The Fifth Level Is Psychological Transformation. At this level, characters engage in self-reflective action. That is, characters develop an understanding of themselves through personal insight and self-awareness. Neo (Keanu Reeves) in *The Matrix* series spends the duration of three movies learning who he really is, particularly in relation to the technological ecosystem in which he finds himself. Through his journey of self-discovery, we also develop an understanding of who we are in relation to the networked, multi-dimensional modern lifestyles we now lead.

The Sixth Level Is Social Transformation. At this level, characters accept new responsibilities with respect to family, community or a group. This happens in two ways. They can shift their attention from a focus on self to a focus on community, or they can shift their allegiance from one community to another as they try to understand where they really belong. There are aspects of previous levels of transformation here, but the focus at this level is negotiating one's relationship with a group. Most of the serial sci-fi dramas that I have watched recently, like *Under the Dome* or *Falling Skies*, feature characters who struggle to understand which social group they truly want to call home, or whether they should simply avoid group affiliation altogether and negotiate life as an individual. As they try to understand whom to trust and which group best represents their ideals and interests, we do as well. Their vacillation provides the kind of story motion that engages us.

The Seventh Level Is Intellectual/Creative Transformation. At this level, story characters solve mysteries and address challenges through education, insight and ingenuity. This describes just about every episode of *Star Trek*. We root for the crew of *The Enterprise* as we adopt their challenges as our own. As they triumph, so do we. At this level, students become heroes of their own learning stories by solving problems, unraveling puzzles and answering questions. Their efforts lead them to new understandings about the world and their roles within it. Creating original work allows them to fully engage in that world. This level translates to personal narrative as well. New understandings and creative approaches to life allow storytellers to create new stories that can guide their future development.

The Eighth Level Is Spiritual Transformation. At this level, characters experience a profound awakening that changes their entire perspective about life on a deep level. Characters emerge reborn in terms of how they see the world and what is truly important. Larry Durrell (Bill Murray) in *Razor's Edge* undergoes such a transformation. Gandhi (Ben Kingsley), in the eponymous movie, seems to have one spiritual revelation after another, which we experience vicariously with him.

One of the great values of thinking about stories in terms of transformation levels is that it facilitates important conversations among teachers and students, mental health clients and counselors, organizational leaders and team members, and whoever is involved in the story development and telling experience. Another value is that it helps us understand the link between transformation and character motivation. Actors looking for guidance will often ask directors, "What motivates my character here?" Understanding the interplay between motive and narrative provides crucial insight about a story.

At its heart, transformation is about realization. I am forever asking story developers, "What does your character realize?" The R word, as I like to call it. Realization doesn't require characters to announce, "Aha, now I get it!" In fact, that sort of blunt force approach to articulating character transformation usually isn't very effective. It is much better for characters to "show their changes rather than tell them" and to embody them in their actions rather than just talk about them. But they do need to realize something. If they don't, then the story has been for naught.

Documentaries: The Art and Science of Telling a True Story

Documentaries are important to anyone who is interested in telling a true story. Bear in mind that documentaries can never be completely true or comprehensive in their presentation. They are often told from a particular perspective and are produced within time limits that compel filmmakers to be selective about the materials they include and exclude. However, documentaries represent our attempt in the media world to distinguish reporting from entertainment. As such, they need to be addressed differently than stories that don't claim to be balanced or accurate.

Much of the media that educators want students to create is non-fiction in nature. Therefore, documentaries are important to them as a media genre. Whether we are creating documentaries, or teaching others to do so, it is important to understand that documentary development is a balancing act. On the one hand we want documentaries to use storytelling structures, like the core and the arc, so that they don't become a disengaging lists of events. One the other, we want them to retain their journalistic integrity and not devolve into entertainment. There are different ways to approach this.

One approach to telling a documentary story is simply to allow the overall "mega event" (a war, an uprising, a research study, whatever) to form the story arc, and to use the unfolding incidents within it to provide the rising and falling action. *Frontline* documentaries often use this approach. An alternative is to blend drama and documentaries to produce what some call docudramas or "mockumentaries." *Narcos*, a dramatic documentary about Pablo Escobar, is a compelling example. It follows the activities of two heroes, or, if you prefer, a protagonist and an antagonist: DEA agent Steve Wagner, played by Boyd Holbrook, and his nemesis Pablo Escobar, played by Wagner Moura. Their two quests work in tandem to outline an overall arc of events. The "outside story" is that Wagner is trying to catch Escobar, while Escobar is trying to elude arrest. The "inside story" is that both battle with their personal demons, and grow and change because of their inner conflicts. We watch both of them evolve in their convictions as they ride the tumultuous zigzag of events. A mockumentary leaves us with a bitter-sweet sense of truth that is more poignant than we experience with typical documentaries. We don't know which parts are journalistically sound and which have been created primarily for entertainment purposes. I will leave an assessment of the value of docudramas, mockumentaries and historical dramatizations up to you.

Another approach to effective documentary presentation is using a narrator to lead the audience through a story, asking the questions that we would ask, and assuming several roles in the process, including storyteller, guide and hero. Morgan Spurlock uses this approach. In his documentary *Supersize Me*, he asks the question, "What would happen if I ate nothing but fast food?" Great question. Although audience members had probably never thought about asking it before, now they are completely focused on answering it. We willingly travel with Spurlock through his many adventures as he seeks the answer to his question so that we can answer what has now become our question. Michael Moore also uses the "narrator as hero" approach. In *Sicko* we travel with him as he explores the question, "Why is healthcare the way it is in America?" His question provides the overall arc for his journey. As he walks through the documentary, his process of discovery leads to answers, which lead to more questions, and so on, zigzagging him, and us, through the story. We remain committed to watching because of the motion it creates. His questions become our questions. We ride the events of the story with him. His transformation becomes ours.

There is another kind of documentary worth mentioning, exemplified by Ron Fricke's *Baraka*. In his work there is none of the conventional narrative we expect to see. Instead, he provides footage of compelling cultural vignettes and breathtaking shots of nature, leaving it up to us to either create a story based on what we see, or make peace with the absence of conventional storytelling. High concept pieces that require the audience to connect all the dots need to present material that is especially compelling. Fricke does a very effective job. However, not everyone who attempts this genre is as successful.

This is just one kind of story that steps outside the mold. Again, I refer you to the chapter about non-conventional approaches to story in my digital storytelling book.

Resolution: The Third Leg of the Story Core

Resolution does not mean a happy ending. It simply means resolving whatever challenges, obstacles or problems had been established during the course of a story–unless, of course, you are planning a sequel. We all know how we feel at the conclusion of a TV program when we see the message "to be continued next week." Arrrgh! We hate that. We may understand the audience engagement and the advertising revenue that it generates, but we still hate it. It is quite acceptable to create stories that leave us with questions that linger or that compel us to ask more questions. But specific story events need to be resolved unless an overwhelming artistic or commercial reason exists not to do so. The narrative human wants closure.

I think that's enough for one presentation. How about showing me one more story arc. Drive that car. Good job! And shall we try to show rising and falling action with the other hand? Okay, probably not. Perhaps it's too late for that.

Calling All Storytellers

I want to thank you for your kind attention, and leave you with the preamble of my storytelling book, which reads as follows:

I have one word for anyone who wants to tell a story, whether it's with computers, with pictures scratched in the sand or solely with the language of the body and the sounds of the human voice. Whether it's the story of a quest to find one's holy-grail, to find oneself or simply to find a way to tell one's story. Whether it's a long story, a short story or a story that never really ends. Whether it's told on the silver screen, in a circle of one's friends, upon the great virtual stage of the World Wide Web or on a hill in full view of the gathered public. Whether it's a personal story, a universal story, someone else's story or a story that can be understood only by the culture that tells it. Whether it's schoolwork, a work of art, art for work or simply something that has to be said.

Whether it's for you, for your friends, for your community or for those you will never meet. Whether it's a personal journey, a scientific adventure, a fantasy of the mind or a memory collage of one's ancestors. Whether it exists as invisible bits of a digital file, as words on paper, as TV reruns or only as memories in the hearts and minds of elders. Whether it never changes, changes every time it is told or changes so slowly that no one notices. I have one word for anyone who wants to tell a story, and that word is: Welcome.

Thank you, and please, go tell your story.

Epilogue- Dancing with the Future

Our innovative selves can't help but have big ideas. It's what we do. Creating new worlds from our imaginations is as much a part of the human condition as our search for meaning.

Our big ideas can get us into trouble or they can save us. The overwhelming presence in our lives of entropy and myopia, and the tendency of our big ideas to produce unanticipated aftershocks, suggest that our big ideas will always do both. We live a story. The rising and falling action of our narrative consists of our innovations, the unintended consequences they generate, and the new ideas we develop to respond to those consequences. Technologies will come and go, but this pattern will never change. It will keep the story forever interesting, dangerous, exciting and inspiring.

How we approach this never-ending story is up to us. We can simply ride the moment, and allow our engagement to keep us anchored to the present, never looking beyond the immediate horizon of our big ideas. Or we can blend our fixation on short-term progress with a long-term perspective, in order to give our forward momentum more purpose and meaning. This approach means that we need to step back from the moment, assess the broader and deeper impacts of our activities, and decide where we want to go ahead of time. We need to let our intentions shape the future.

This, then, is the dance: We need to love the moment, but also need to guide our movements using our wiser selves who understand that today's actions can echo for an eternity. We need to approach the present with a vision for what an eternity should look like.

And we need to do this now. The future is just getting started, and it needs our big ideas. Let's tell stories that are filled with big ideas that celebrate not just our progress and innovation, but also our wisdom and stewardship. Let's dance in ways that are truly worthy of our imaginations.

References

Cover

1.   Image of boy with globe. Used through a paid subscription from Clipart.com.

2.   Image of Clouds. (n.d.) Through a paid subscription from Clipart.com.

New Words for Now Media

1.   Transmersive is a term developed by Monica Helms.

Idea 1– Writing Te(ch)xt – Now Media, New Literacies

1.   Bush, G. (2010, January 16). *Rarely is the Question Asked...* [Video recording]. Retrieved from: https://www.youtube.com/watch?v=-ej7ZEnjSeA.

2.   Picture of Miss Phelps, Jason Ohler, from class picture, 1958. Author unknown.

3.   Picture of John Hasselback and Jason Ohler, from high school yearbook, no attribution cited. Presumably pictures were taken by photography students.

4.   Sherry Turkle. (2006). *Always-On/Always-On-You: The Tethered Self, Handbook of Mobile Communications and Social Change*, James Katz (ed.). Cambridge, MA: MIT Press.

5.   McLuhan, Eric; McLuhan, Marshall; Hutchon, Kathryn. *City as Classroom*. (1977). Toronto: McLuhan Associates Limited.

6.   McLuhan, M. (1964). *Understanding Media*. New York: New American Library.

7.   Photo of young woman in park with laptop. (n.d.) Through a paid subscription from Clipart.com.

8. Scorsese, M. (2013). *Persistence of Vision: Reading the Language of Cinema*. National Endowment for the Humanities Wards & Honors: 2013 Jefferson Lecture. Retrieved from: http://www.neh.gov/about/awards/jefferson-lecture/martin-scorsese-lecture

9. Lucas, G. (n.d.). Quoted in: Daly, J. (2004, September). *Life on the Screen: Visual Literacy in Education*. Edutopia. Retrieved from: http://www.edutopia.org/life-screen.

10. Rosling, H. (n.d., uploaded 2010). *200 Countries, 200 Years, 4 Minutes*. Retrieved from: http://www.gapminder.org/videos/200-years-that-changed-the-world-bbc.

11. Ohler, J. (2010). *Digital Community, Digital Citizen*. Thousand Oaks: Corwin Press.

12. Dertouzos, M. (2001). *The Unfinished Revolution: Human-centered Computers and What They Can Do for Us*. New York: HarperCollins.

13. Goodman, S. (2003). *Teaching Youth Media: A Critical Guide to Literacy, Video Making and Social Change*. New York: Teachers College Press.

14. Egan, K. (1986). *Teaching as Storytelling*. Chicago: University of Chicago Press.

15. Bledsoe G., and Molalla Elementary students. (n.d., uploaded 2007). *How to Animate a Rolling Ball*. Retrieved from: https://www.youtube.com/watch?v=cgbLAreElNI.

16. Good, C. (n.d.). *Aggressive Driver*. Clay Good's personal collection. Used with permission.

Idea 2 – Digital Citizenship – Ethics During Times of Extreme Change

1. Turkle, S. Ibid.

2. Image of microwave. (n.d.) Used through a paid subscription from Clipart.com.

3. Ribble, M. (2013). *Digital Citizenship in Schools*. Eugene: ISTE.

4. Collins, J. (1953). *The Mind of Kierkegaard.* Princeton, NJ: Princeton University Press.

5. Ohler. Ibid.

6. Kay, A. (1980s). Quote appeared during a Hong Kong Press Conference during the 1980s. Retrieved from: https://en.wikiquote.org/wiki/Alan_Kay

7. PhotoShopped example of Jason Ohler, before and after. (1993, approx.) Original photographer unknown. Image manipulation by Ohler, J.

8. Rachel Adatto, quoted in, Rubin, S. (2013, January 4). *Israel tells underweight models to gain weight or get off the runway.* Christian Science Monitor. Retrieved from: http://www.csmonitor.com/World/Middle-East/2013/0104/Israel-tells-underweight-models-to-gain-weight-or-get-off-the-runway

Idea 3 – Five Trends that Bend – Technological Trajectories that Will Change Everything

1. Entman, L. (2014, Mar 14). *Electric Thinking Cap Controls Learning Speed.* Retrieved from: http://news.vanderbilt.edu/2014/03/thinking-cap/

2. Heck, C. (2015, Feb 13). *Could This 'Thinking Cap' Help You Learn?* Live Science. http://www.livescience.com/49815-can-a-thinking-cap-help-you-learn.html

3. Photo of Math Hat. CC license. From Elsevier. Retrieved from: http://www.sciencedirect.com/science/article/pii/S0960982213004867

4. New York Times staff. (1923, March 18). *Climbing Mount Everest Is Work For Supermen."* Quote by Edmund Hillary. New York: New York Times.

5. Image of hero, infographic combination. Hero: Used through a paid subscription from Clipart.com. Infographic (n.d.). QMEE. Used with permission from QMEE. Retrieved from: http://blog.qmee.com/online-in-60-seconds-infographic-a-year-later/.

6. Weinschenk, S. (2012, Sep 11). *Why We're All Addicted to Texts, Twitter and Google.* Retrieved from: https://www.

psychologytoday.com/blog/brain-wise/201209/why-were-all-addicted-texts-twitter-and-google

7. Fallon. C. (2015, September 1). *33 Can't-Miss New Books You'll Want To Curl Up With This Fall.* Huffington Post. Retrieved from: http://www.huffingtonpost.com/entry/2015-fall-books-preview_55e072fae4b0b7a96338a345

8. Campbell, J. (2008). *The Hero with a Thousand Faces.* Novato: New World Library.

9. Photo of 737. Creative Commons license. Retrieved from: https://commons.wikimedia.org/wiki/Category:User:AVIA_BavARia/uploads/flickr/78023771@N00#/media/File:Checking_the_engine_%288557695912%29.jpg

10. Tarantola, A. (2012, Feb. 16). *'5D' discs can store data until well after the sun burns out.* Engadget. http://www.engadget.com/2016/02/16/5d-discs-can-store-data-until-well-after-the-sun-burns-out/

11. McLuhan, M. Ibid.

12. Livestats internet traffic report. (2015, October 5). Retrieved from: http://www.internetlivestats.com/

13. Schonfeld, E. (2008, January 9). *Google Processing 20,000 Terabytes A Day, And Growing.* Techcrunch. Retrieved from: http://techcrunch.com/2008/01/09/google-processing-20000-terabytes-a-day-and-growing/

14. Kelly, J. (2012, May 21). *Taming Big Data [A Big Data Infographic].* Wikibon Blog. Retrieved from: http://wikibon.org/blog/taming-big-data/

15. Pariser, E. (2011). *The Filter Bubble.* London: Penguin.

16. Negroponte. N. (1995). *Being Digital.* New York: Knopf.

17. Ohler, J. (2001). *Then What?* Juneau: Brinton Books.

18. Kramer, A.; Guillory, J.; Hancock, J. (2014). *Experimental Evidence of Massive-scale Emotional Contagion through Social Networks.* Proceedings of the National Academy of Sciences, vol. 111 no. 24. Retrieved from: http://www.pnas.org/content/111/24/8788.full

19. McCambridge, R. (2014, April 22). *Gates' $100M Philanthropic Venture inBloom Dies after Parents Say "No Way"*. NonProfit Quarterly. Retrieved from: https://nonprofitquarterly.org/2014/04/22/gates-100m-philanthropic-venture-inbloom-dies-after-parents-say-no-way/

20. Image: VR + RL diagram. Creative Commons license.

21. Paintings by Kate Karafotas. Used with permission of the artist. Part of a Grade 8 Visual arts project called Inner Dialogue at the International School of Prague.

22. Photo of woman at lighthouse. Used through a paid subscription from Clipart.com.

23. Photo of Kissing Bot. (2011, May 2). Used with permission from Digital Media Division, Digitized Information Inc. Retrieved from: http://www.diginfo.tv/v/11-0090-r-en.php

24. Walter, G. (2015, Dec 3). *Florida Woman's Car Turned Her in for a Hit-and-Run*. Future Tense. http://www.slate.com/blogs/future_tense/2015/12/03/a_florida_woman_s_car_turned_her_in_for_a_hit_and_run.html

25. Gokey, M. (2015, July 30). *Apple patents a crazy stylus that senses texture to make 3D files*. Digital Trends. Retrieved from: http://www.digitaltrends.com/mobile/apple-stylus-patent-texture/

26. Hicks, J. (2015, March 2). *Johnnie Walker Smart Bottle Debuts At Mobile World Congress*. Forbes. Retrieved from: http://www.forbes.com/sites/jenniferhicks/2015/03/02/johnnie-walker-smart-bottle-debuts-at-mobile-world-congress/

27. Venter, C. (2010, May). *Ted Talk: Craig Venter: Watch me unveil "synthetic cell"*. Retrieved from: http://www.ted.com/talks/craig_venter_unveils_synthetic_life#t-8562

28. Zhang, R. (2016, Feb 1). DNA Got a Kid Kicked Out of School—And It'll Happen Again. Science. Retrieved from: http://www.wired.com/2016/02/schools-kicked-boy-based-dna/?mbid=nl_ozy

29. Macdonald, A. (Producer), &, Garland, A. (Director). (2015). *Ex Machina* [Motion Picture]. United Kingdom: Universal Studios.

30. *Watson (computer).* (n.d.) Wikipedia. https://en.wikipedia. org/wiki/Watson_(computer)#References

31. Ulanoff, L. (2016, Jan 27). *A computer beat a champion of the strategy game Go for the first time. Mashable.* http://www.wired. com/2016/01/in-a-huge-breakthrough-googles-ai-beats-a-top-player-at-the-game-of-go/?mbid=nl_12716

32. Profis, S. (2010, April 14). *Your hoodie just updated your Facebook page.* C|NET. Retrieved from: http://www.cnet.com/news/your-hoodie-just-updated-your-facebook-page/

33. Zolfagharifard, E. (2014, January 28). T*he novel that really is a spine-chiller! WEARABLE book lets you physically feel characters' emotions as you read.* Daily Mail. Retrieved from: http://www.dailymail.co.uk/sciencetech/article-2547524/The-novel-really-spine-chiller-WEARABLE-book-lets-physically-feel-characters-emotions-read.html

34. Palmer, S. (2014, December 6). *CES Trend Spotting: Inconspicuous Innovation.* Shelly Palmer site. Retrieved from: http://www.shellypalmer.com/2015/12/ces-trendspotting-inconspicuous-innovation/

35. Hutchinson, A. (2016, March). *How a Fitbit May Make You a Fit Fit.* New York Times Sunday Review - Opinion retrieved: http://www.nytimes.com/2016/03/20/opinion/sunday/how-a-fitbit-may-make-you-a-bit-fit.html?smprod=nytcore-iphone&smid=nytcore-iphone-share

36. Rabin, A. (Producer), Schiller, V. (Producer). (2015). *Dark Net: Upgrade* [Documentary]. Showtime, Vocativ Films.

37. Spangler, T. (2014, October 29). *Movie Industry Officially Bans Google Glass, Other Wearable Devices.* Variety. Retrieved from: http://variety.com/2014/digital/news/movie-industry-officially-bans-google-glass-other-wearable-devices-1201342303/

38. Kring. T. (2009, October 10). *Heroes Creator on Transmedia Storytelling.* [Interviewed by Scott Kirsner.] Retrieved from: http://www.youtube.com/watch?v=jWyo00IoXo8

39. Jenkins, H. (2009, February 11). *If It Doesn't Spread, It's Dead. (Part One): Media Viruses and Memes.* Aca-Fan blog. Retrieved from: http://henryjenkins.org/2009/02/if_it_doesnt_spread_its_dead_p.html

40. Kurzweil, R. (2005). *The Singularity is Near*. New York: Penguin.

Idea 4 – The Art of the Story – Telling Your Story, Owning Your Narrative

1. McKee, R. (1997). *Story- Substance, Structure, Style, and Principles of Screenwriting.* New York: Regan Books.

2. Duarte, N. (2010, November 11). *Nancy Duarte: The Secret Structure of Great Talks* [Video file]. Retrieved from: https://www.youtube.com/watch?v=1nYFpuc2Umk

3. Officialpsy. (2012, July 15). *Gangnam Style* [Video file]. Retrieved from: https://www.youtube.com/watch?v=9bZk-p7q19f0

4. Schmidt, C. (2007, June 7 uploaded). *Charlie Schmidt's Keyboard Cat! - THE ORIGINAL!* [Video file]. Retrieved from: https://www.youtube.com/watch?v=J---aiyznGQ

5. Gazzaniga, M. (n.d.). *Split brain behavioral experiments* [Video file]. Retrieved from: https://www.youtube.com/watch?v=ZM-LzP1VCANo

6. Dertouzos, M. Ibid.

7. Olshansky, B. (n.d.) *Time for a Paradigm Shift: Recognizing the Critical Role of Pictures Within Literacy Learning.* Bankstreet. Retrieved from: https://www.bankstreet.edu/occasional-paper-series/31/part-iii/time-for-a-paradigm-shift/

8. Einstein quote. (n.d.). Retrieved from: http://www.brainyquote.com/quotes/quotes/a/alberteins109805.html

9. Theodosakis, N. (2009). *The Director in the Classroom.* Penticton, BC: published by the author.

INDEX

Internet of Everything; IoE, 117-118, 144, 154
Internet of Things; IoT, 45, 117, 146, 151
iPad, 109
IPF, Idiopathic Pulmonary Fibrosis, 4-5
IR (immersive reality), 13-16, 22, 27, 40, 55, 58, 67-68, 79, 86, 117-118,
      135-136, 139, 141-142, 144, 156, 160, 167, 204
ISTE (International Society of Technology in Education), 59
iStuff, 156, 173
Ivey, Jonathan, 162-163
iWatch, 157

Jackson, Michael, 145
Jason Ohlers, many on the Internet, 113
Jenkins, Henry, 166
Jeopardy, (Friedman) 138, 152
Jobs, Steve, 196
Johnny Walker smart labeling, 147

Kasparov, Garry, 152
Karafotas, Kate; Inner Dialogue artist, 137
Kawasaki, Guy, 87
Kay, Alan, 76
Kierkegaard, Søren, 63
Kinect, Microsoft's, 108-109, 136
King, Martin Luther, 196
Kingsley, Ben (Gandhi), 196
Kissing bot, 138-139, 160
Kring, Tim, 166
Kurzweil, Ray, 161, 170

LinkedIn, 94, 113
Lists vs. stories. 41, 187, 199, 200, 203
Literacy, illiteracy, all of Idea 1 (1-49); 97, 99, 144, 167,-168, 205-206, 209,
      221
Long hair, as an issue in the 1960s, 8
Lucas, George, 29
Lung transplant, my double, 5, 147

Magic Leap, 136
Math hat, the, 98, 115, 162-163, 170
Matrix, The (Silver), 137, 224
McLuhan, Eric, 15
McLuhan, Marshall, 15, 26, 96, 124

Nielsen, Connie (Lucilla), 223
Norma Rae (Sally Field), 224
Now media, 12, 21-24, 27, 57, 118, 167, 206, 220
Nowist, 37, 63

OAC (Open Access Course), 154
Obi-Wan Kenobi, 135
Online anthropology, 72
Optical storage, 127
Ordinary People (Schwary), 177
Ouriginal work, ouriginal, ouriginalize, 81
Outstanders vs. bystanders, 103

Palmer, Shelly, 162
Parents; parents, my, 7-8, 33, 41, 65-71, 79, 88, 91, 94, 109, 115, 132, 149-
       150, 157, 175, 217,
Pariser, Eli, 128
Partycipation, 55-57
Pavlov, Ivan, 116
Petabyte storage, 125
Photoshop, 23, 100, 102, 113, 216
Plato, 77
Predictive analytics, 128-129
Princess Leia, 135
Privacy, 74-76, 90, 141
Production values, 182, 208, 217-221

Quantified Self (QS), The, 19
Queen, the, 102

Radios; radios, early, 25, 157,
Razor's Edge, (Fairbairn), 225
RFID (Radio Frequency IDentification), 160-161
Recording script, narrative, 216-217
Reed, Oliver (Proximo), 223
Relatability, 188-189
Revealer, the, 109-110
Ribble, Mike, 62, 71
RL (Real Life), 13-16, 29, 31, 43, 55, 57, 59, 62-64, 68, 72, 79, 117, 135-
       136, 139, 141, 144, 148, 156, 161, 166-167, 189.
Road Warrior (Byron Kennedy), 224
Roadrunner (Warner Bros.), 195
Robot(s), robotics, 36, 39, 48, 74, 106, 153, 170, 193, 222

tEcosystem, 55
TED talks, 3, 118, 120, 129, 149, 196
Tell, William, 173-178, 182, 188, 223
Terabyte storage, 123-125
Texture sensing, transferring stylus, 146
Then What? (Ohler), 55, 130, 133, 173
Theosodakis, Nikos, 213
THINK (acronym), 89
Thinking caps, 36, 67-70,
Toronto, University of, 15, 96 124
Transformation, in narrative; personal, 35, 42-43, 79, 95, 121, 173, 177-
179, 182-187, 198, 201, 203, 213, 223-228,
Transmedia, transmedia storytelling, 20-21, 118, 165-169, 204-206
Transmersion, transmersive, 20, 167-168, 220
Turkle, Sherry, 14, 55, 57
Twitter, 20, 113, 166, 199, 214
Tyrannosaurus Tom, 7

Uber, 107, 148
Under the Dome (Vaughn), 225
UW3; University of the World Wide Web, 14, 17
UOPS, 80-82

Vanderbilt University's Visual Cognitive Neuroscience Laboratory, 114
VDT (Visually Differentiated Text), 33
Venter, Craig, 149
VHS storage, 125
Visual literacy, 28, 205
Visual portrait of the story (VPS), 212
Voice-over narration, 42, 208, 213
VR (virtual reality), 62, 79, 106, 114, 135

Watson (by IBM), 152
Wearware, 156, 160
Web 1.0, 143-144
Web 2.0, 143-146
Web 2.1, 143
Web 3, 117, 144-146, 155-156
Web 4 (Web of Things, IoT), 45,117, 144-146, 151, 155
Websters, 143
WI-FI, 157-160
Wiki, 34, 47, 143
Wikipedia, 48, 145